£6.99

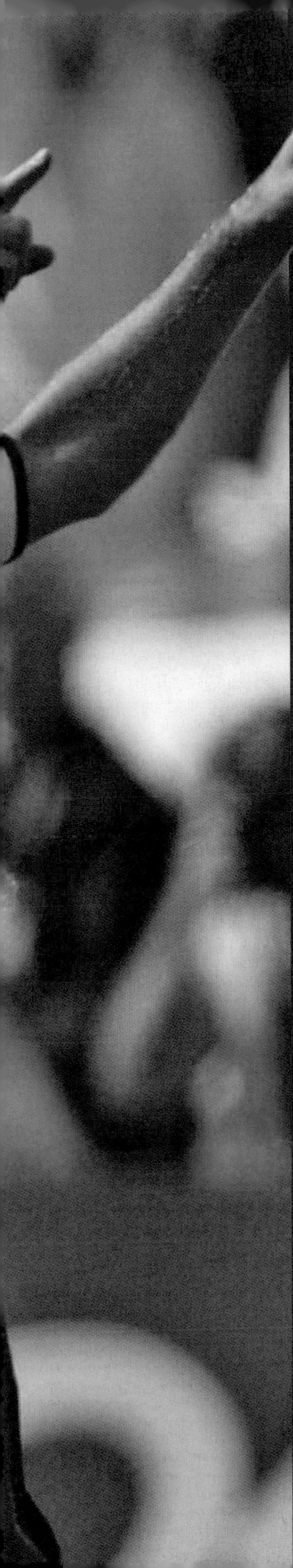

Contents

UNOFFICIAL

Written by Ken Kenilworth

This is an unofficial, unauthorised and independent publication. Reference to David Beckham is a reference to the subject matter of this product. It does not purport to indicate trade origin connected with David Beckham nor anyone acting for or associated with him. Neither David Beckham nor anyone acting for or associated with him have given their permission to publish this book. Whilst the publishers believe all content of this publication to be true at the time of publishing it they do not accept any responsibility in this regard. To contact the publisher, do so at City Forum, 250 City Road, London EC1V 2QQ. Ref ZN7.

Printed in the E.U.

Real Life Superstar

DAVID BECKHAM

New stars rise in the world of football every season, but only a few endure – and England's captain David Beckham tops the list of those who do.

Having recently celebrated his 30th birthday, David has been a glamorous superstar for almost a decade now – and not only on the soccer pitch.

From the time he first emerged onto the Premiership scene in England to his current status as one of the world's most valued players, he has developed as a style leader and entertainment icon. He is adored and idolised all over the world, by fans young and old.

This David Beckham Unofficial Annual celebrates the life and times of a true footballing great...

We hope you enjoy reading it...

Action Man

Let's begin with some great shots of David playing for England...

Action Man

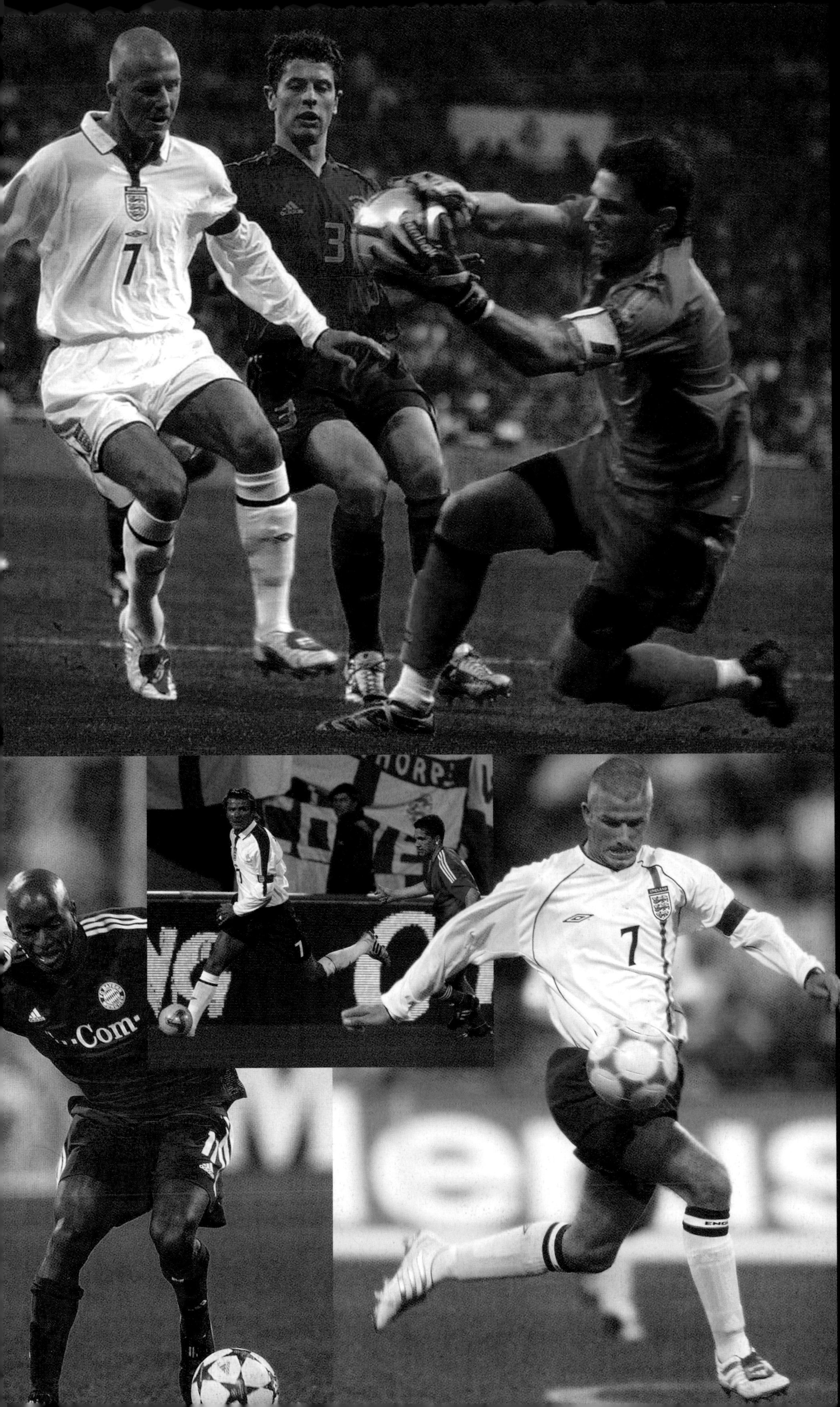

The Story of a Footballer

BOY WONDER

Like father like son, as they say.

David Beckham's dad, Ted, was a lifelong Manchester United fan, so it was entirely natural that the youngster should follow in his father's footsteps. As the boy grew up he followed United's progress avidly and hero-worshipped the club's great players – especially skipper Bryan Robson who was also captain of England.

Little did he know it, but young David was destined to play alongside 'Captain Marvel' one day – and would perform a similar inspirational role to his hero, both in United's

dazzling future and in the colours of his country.

David's parents always kept him supplied with the latest replica version of United's famous red, white and black strip. He even wore a Man U shirt when invited to train with Spurs (the White Hart Lane club had been hearing very good things about the promising schoolboy footballer from Leytonstone).

Indeed, David was such a fine young player that he won the finals of the Bobby Charlton Soccer Skills Championship, doing so with a record haul of points. His reward was a two-week visit to the Nou

Camp Stadium, home of Barcelona in Spain. There, the talented youngster met Barca's trio of famous Brits: Welsh international Mark Hughes, Scottish cap Steve Archibald and England's super-striker Gary Lineker.

Who knew that young David was destined to one day play against Barcelona in the world famous Nou Camp and in the colours of their greatest rivals, Real Madrid?!

Back home, the would-be soccer star reached yet another milestone in his life, when selected as Man United's mascot for a Premier League match against West Ham. Chest puffed out with pride he marched onto the Upton Park pitch with Bryan Robson, and even had a kick-about with his great hero during the pre-match warm-up.

As the talented boy grew he simply got better and better as a footballer. With each passing match he played in, it seemed inevitable that he would one day turn professional.

Spurs retained their interest in him and would undoubtedly have snapped him up – if Manchester

DB PERSONAL FILE
Full Name: David Robert Beckham
Birthdate: 2 May 1975
Birthplace: Leytonstone, East London
Starsign: Taurus
Height: 5'11"
Weight: 11st 8lbs
Wife: Victoria
Sons: Brooklyn, Romeo and Cruz
Homes: Hertfordshire, England and Madrid, Spain

United hadn't made a timely approach. When their offer came, the matter was settled with barely a second thought and David signed as an Associated Schoolboy with the Old Trafford club. At 16 he left home to become an official Man U Trainee.

Under the watchful eyes of Old Trafford's wise and wily coaching staff, his progress was rapid. And he soon had the first of many honours under his belt – an FA Youth Cup winners' medal when United beat Crystal Palace with a 6-3 aggregate in the 1992 final. David scored the second goal in United's 3-1 win in the first-leg and then starred in the second-leg. It was the club's first success in this prestigious competition for 28 years.

DB CLUB 'DEBUTS'

Football League debut: for Preston North End v Doncaster Rovers on 4 March 1995, while on loan

For Manchester United: 23 September 1992 as a sub v Brighton in League Cup 2nd Round Premier League debut – for Manchester United v Leeds United on 2 April 1995 at Villa Park For Real Madrid: v Mallorca in Spanish Super Cup 1st leg on 24 August 2003

La Liga debut: for Real Madrid v Real Betis on 30 August 2003

BREAKING THROUGH

In September 1992, young Beckham sat pensively on the bench during United's First Round UEFA Cup tie against Torpedo Moscow at Old Trafford. But he wasn't called into the action on that occasion. His senior debut came a few days later when Alex Ferguson sent him on as a 70th minute substitute for Andrei Kanchelskis in a 1-1 draw with Brighton in the Second Round of the Coca-Cola Cup competition.

United's boss was so impressed with young Becks that, four months later, he offered him a professional contract. Naturally, the ambitious youngster was delighted to accept this golden opportunity. There were nearly two more years spent learning his trade before he was selected again for first-team duty. The Coca-Cola Cup again provided the opportunity, on 21 September 1994, and Port Vale provided the opposition at Vale Park where United won 2-1.

He made his Old Trafford debut in the return-leg on 5 October and it was from his corner-kick that David May netted United's second goal in a 2-0 win that rounded off a 4-1 aggregate victory.

David Beckham's career milestones came thick-and-fast after that. He netted his first goal for United in a 4-0 European Champions League win against the Turkish champions Galatasary at Old Trafford on 7 December 1994. His

FA Cup debut came on 28 January 1995, in a 5-2 Fourth Round victory over Wrexham.

To boost his experience, United loaned David to Third Division Preston North End in March '95 and he made his Football League debut under manager Gary Peters, against Doncaster Rovers at Deepdale. That match, a 2-2 draw, also brought his first goal in League soccer. He stayed with the Deepdale club for four more games, scoring again in the next match, against

Fulham at Deepdale and being hugely impressive against Bury, Exeter and Lincoln.

Back at Old Trafford David found himself in serious contention for a first-team place and his Premier League debut came in a 0-0 draw at home to Leeds United in front of almost 44,000 fans. He also made inroads on the international front, making his Under-21 debut against Brazil in the Toulon Tournament in France, the first of his nine Under-21 caps.

DOUBLE DELIGHT – 1995-96

The 1995-96 season was the one in which David really blossomed. He made 37 Premier League appearances and scored seven goals as United saw off Newcastle's title challenge. The Old Trafford club also reached that season's FA Cup final, thanks in part to David's winning strike against Chelsea in the semi-final at Villa Park.

The 1996 FA Cup final, against Liverpool at Wembley, was settled by a magnificent piece of quick thinking by United's French superstar Eric Cantona who netted the only goal of the game.

The result meant David had collected a Premier League champions medal and an FA Cup winner's medal in his first full season as a senior player – a magnificent achievement for a 21-year-old.

GOAL OF THE CENTURY – 1996-97

David made a fantastic start to the 1996-97 Premier League campaign, scoring his famous 'halfway line goal' for United against Wimbledon at Selhurst Park. It was a fabulous strike that will never be forgotten, especially by Dons' 'keeper Neil Sullivan. The wonder goal, which came late in the game, completed a 3-0 victory for the visitors.

The strike also raised young Beckham's profile within the game – and helped convince national

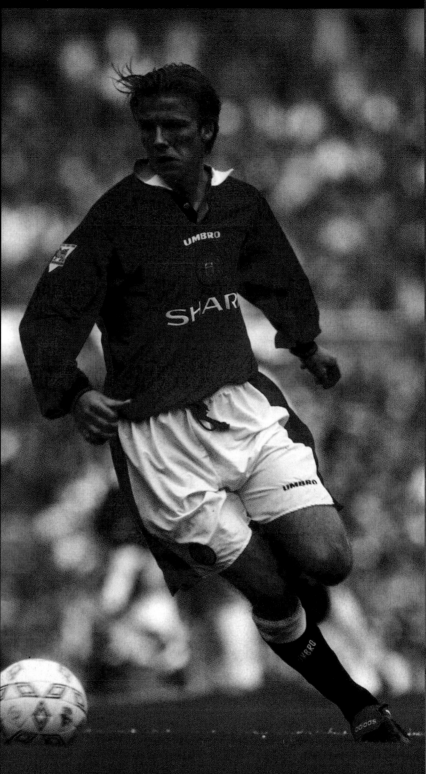

coach Glenn Hoddle to select him for a World Cup qualifier against Moldova in Chisinau that September. David's full international debut finished in a 3-0 victory for the Three Lions side. After that he became more and more involved as England gradually edged closer to qualification for the 1998 World Cup finals.

On the club front United were eliminated relatively early in the two domestic cup competitions and they reached the semi-finals in the European Champions' League. But the team dominated the Premiership table, finished seven points ahead of Newcastle and added yet another medal to David's collection.

DB FIRST GOALS
For Manchester United:
v Galatasary on
7 December 1994 in
European Cup
Football League goal: –
for Preston North End
v Doncaster Rovers on
4 March 1995, while
on loan
La Liga goal: – for Real
Madrid v Real Betis on
30 August 2003
For England: v Colombia
on 26 June 1998

BECKHAM'S BLIP – 1997-98

Arsenal won the Premier League title and the FA Cup in 1997-98. Real Madrid won the European Champions' League. But Manchester United won nothing at all, although they were serious contenders on all fronts and David was fully involved along the way.

These disappointments were well and truly behind him when he travelled to France as a member of Glenn Hoddle's World Cup squad. Having starred in England's qualifying tournament, it was fully expected that he would be an obvious choice for the team's first match against Tunisia. In the event he spent the entire game on the subs' bench, watching England win 2-0.

His non-selection led to a heated discussion with the coach, who assured the player that he would have an integral part to play in the competition.

Yet Beckham was still warming the bench as the second game, versus Romania, kicked-off. He got his chance in the 33rd minute replacing the injured Paul Ince. Despite David's enlivening presence, England relinquished control of a game that should have been in the bag and lost 2-1.

Hoddle's side now had to secure a point from their last Group game, against Colombia, to ensure a passage to the Second Stage. This time David was in the starting line-up. Darren Anderton opened the scoring on 20 minutes. Ten minutes later Becks made his first mark on the tournament with his first goal for England, a real stunner from one of his trademark free-kicks.

England went on to a Second Round meeting with Argentina – and that's when 'Beckham's Blip' occurred. Early in the second half with the score-line standing at two-all, he was sent sprawling by Argentine star Diego Simeone and the referee blew for a free-kick. As he lay prone on the ground, David lashed out at Simeone and was promptly red-carded for the action.

Without him the game went into extra-time and then to a penalty shoot-out - won by Argentina who went on to meet Holland in the quarter finals.

Back home, many devastated England fans blamed David's rash action for England's exit and he suddenly found himself at the lowest ebb of his career.

BOUNCING BACK – 1998-99

David began the 1998-99 season determined to shake off his World Cup woes. After some initial barracking at away matches the bad memory gradually subsided and, ironically enough, the bitter experience in France seemed to make him a better, stronger player.

It was back to business as usual with Manchester United who were also determined to turn their fortunes around following their trophy-less campaigns of 1997-98. And what a turnaround it turned out to be!

As United forged ahead on three fronts David played his part to the full. In the Premier League things went right down to the wire and, on the last day, United and Arsenal were neck-and-neck.

To secure the title the Red Devils had to beat Tottenham at Old Trafford in their final game of the Premiership programme. Spurs opened the scoring but David equalised just before half-time, with his sixth goal of the campaign. Two minutes after the interval Andy Cole made the all-important strike that tied up the title for United.

On the following weekend they met Newcastle in the FA Cup final at Wembley. An early blow came when Roy Keane was injured. His replacement, Teddy Sheringham, had the ball in the net within seconds of coming on. Alex

Ferguson reshuffled his pack with David now controlling the centre of midfield and a later goal from Paul Scholes gave United a 2-0 victory, the FA Cup and their second 'double' in three seasons.

A few days later, United had an unprecedented 'treble' in their sights when they met Bayern Munich in the European Champions' League final in Barcelona. But, with the game in injury-time, it looked as though the treble-dream was over as the German side was leading by a single goal.

Then United won a

corner. David took it. The ball found Ryan Giggs. His shot was blocked, but Teddy Sheringham was once again on hand to side-foot an equaliser.

With extra-time looming, United forced another corner. Again Beckham took it. Sheringham received the ball and flicked it on to Ole Gunnar Solskjaer who netted the winner. The historic treble was completed.

David had three more medals in his trophy cabinet – and his 'blip' was long forgotten.

DB CLUB HONOURS

WITH MANCHESTER UNITED
Premier League Championship: 1995-96, 1996-97, 1998-99, 1999-2000, 2000-01, 2002-03
Premier League Runners-up: 1997-98
FA Cup Winner: 1996, 1999
League Cup Runners-up: 2003
Charity Shield Winners: 1996, 1997
Charity Shield Runners-up: 1998, 1999, 2000, 2001
European Champions' Cup Winner: 1999
FA Youth Cup Winner: 1992

WITH REAL MADRID
Spanish Cup Runners-up: 2004

UPS & DOWNS – 1999-2000

Try as they might, the Treble Winners had no chance of repeating the feat in 1999-2000. For a start they didn't even compete for the FA Cup. The game's authorities insisted they participate instead in January 2000's eight-team FIFA World Club Championship in Brazil – a worthy but somewhat meaningless competition in which they did not do particularly well. David appeared in two of United's three matches there.

Two months earlier he had played for United in the annual World Club Championship game in Tokyo, against South American title-holders Palmeiras. A 1-0 victory, courtesy of Roy Keane's 35th minute goal, made Manchester United the first British club to be crowned 'World Club Champions'.

David did not play when Aston Villa eliminated United from the League Cup in the Third Round. But he was fully involved in a Premier League campaign dominated by the Red Devils. They netted no less than 32 goals in the last nine matches of the season and secured the title with a game left to play.

On the international front he continued doing his bit for England under new coach Kevin Keegan. After finishing second in their European Championship qualifying race the team met Scotland in a two-legged play-off. Both sides enjoyed away victories in the tie, but England went to the finals in Belgium and Holland thanks to a 2-1 aggregate.

Unfortunately, the Euro finals proved a huge disappointment to Keegan's squad. Despite a hugely satisfying win against Germany – England's first tournament win against them since the 1966 World Cup final – Qualifying Group defeats by Romania and Portugal meant an early flight home.

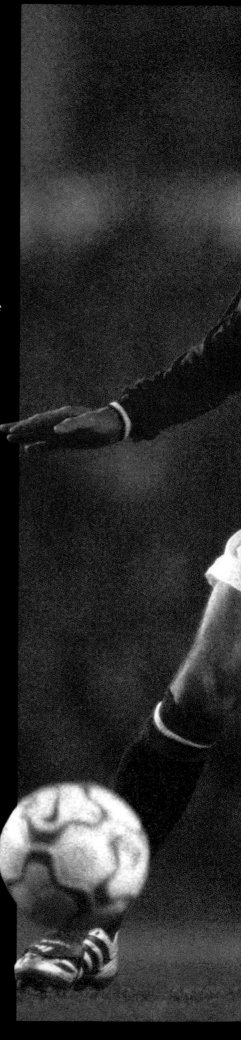

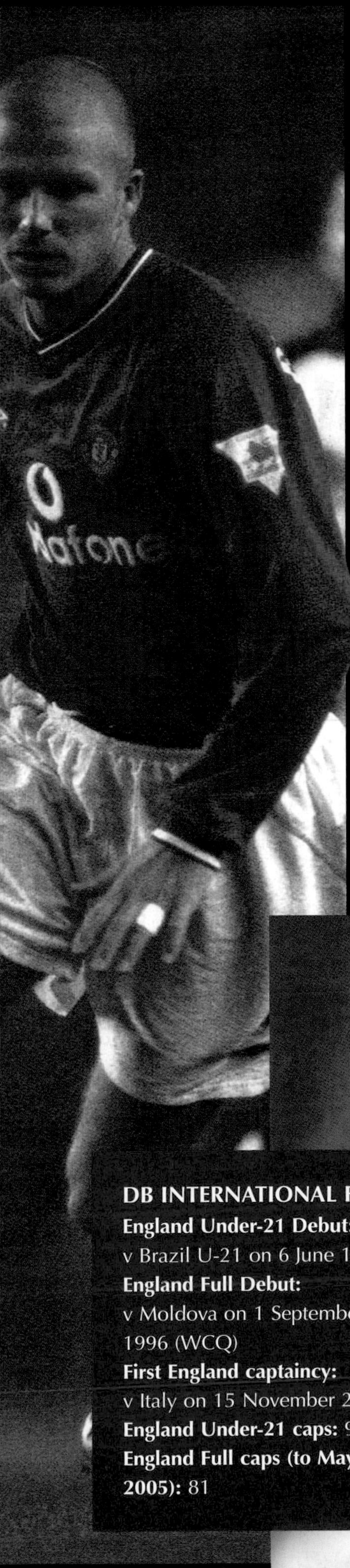

THE MAN IN THE ARMBAND – 2000-01

Kevin Keegan's reign as England's coach ended after a disappointing 1-0 defeat by Germany in the last match at 'old' Wembley before the famous stadium was demolished to make way for the magnificent new venue due to open in 2006.

Howard Wilkinson next saw the team through a World Cup qualifying draw with Finland, in which David did not participate. He was back, however, for the next fixture – a friendly encounter with Italy in Turin on 15 November 2000.

A new caretaker manager, Peter Taylor, was now in charge and it was he who made one of the finest decisions in Three Lions history by appointing David Captain of the team. Beckham would go on to wear the armband under new coach Sven-Goran Eriksson whose reign began in February 2001 with a 3-0 friendly win against Spain at Villa Park.

David proved an excellent leader as England battled for a place in the 2002 World Cup finals, to be staged in Korea and Japan.

Meanwhile, Manchester United were heading for a third successive Premiership triumph, David playing his part to the full with 31 appearances and nine goals in the campaign. This time the Red Devils completed the task in hand with no less than five games still to go. Shortly after securing the national title they were eliminated from the European Champions' League by Bayern Munich in the quarter-finals.

DB INTERNATIONAL FILE

England Under-21 Debut:
v Brazil U-21 on 6 June 1995
England Full Debut:
v Moldova on 1 September 1996 (WCQ)
First England captaincy:
v Italy on 15 November 2000
England Under-21 caps: 9
England Full caps (to May 2005): 81

WORLD CUP DRAMAS – 2001-02

Manchester United's defence of the Premier League title finally floundered in 2001-02. After allowing Arsenal to overtake them in March they eventually finished third (the Gunners went on to complete the League & FA Cup double). In Europe, United reached the Champions' League semi-finals before elimination by Bayer Leverkusen.

It was in a World Cup qualifier against Germany in Munich in September 2001 that David and the England team made a sensational impact. He led the lads quite brilliantly and was involved in the build up to four of the goals in a famous and celebrated 5-1 victory.

He was brilliant in the next game too, as England crushed Albania in Newcastle. In the end it all boiled down to a crunch meeting with Greece at Old Trafford on 6 October 2001. To avoid the play-offs, England had to equal or better Germany's result against Finland in a match played at the same time.

While Germany were drawing with the Finns, Greece went ahead twice in Manchester, putting England on the back-foot. It was David who inspired the side in its hour of need with one of his finest performances in a Three Lions shirt. With less than two minutes to go, he took a free-kick which flew into the net for the vital equaliser that took England to the finals and consigned Germany to the play-offs.

David was soon in the news again, but for an entirely different reason. In a European Champions' League meeting with Deportivo La Coruna at Old Trafford in April he sustained a broken bone in his foot and was in danger of missing the World Cup finals altogether.

Thankfully, some excellent medical care pulled him through in time to travel with the team to Japan and to line-up in the first game against Sweden in Saitama, which ended in a 1-1 draw. Next came a famous 1-0 victory against Argentina in Sapporo – the goal coming from David's expertly taken spot-kick just before half-time. Then a 0-0 draw with Nigeria sent England into a Second Round meeting with Denmark in Niigata which resulted in a Beckham-inspired 3-0 win.

Mighty Brazil were next up in the quarter-finals in Shizuoka. On 50 minutes, with the scoreline delicately poised at 1-1, they were awarded a free-kick some four yards outside the English penalty area. As Ronaldinho lined-up to take the kick he spotted David Seaman off his line. Quick as a flash, the Brazilian ace lobbed the ball over the stranded 'keeper and into the net for a 2-1 victory. Ouch!

THE TRANSFER – 2002-03

The Beckham rumour mill was working at full tilt in 2002-03 – especially after Fergie's famous dressing room tantrum when United were eliminated by arch-rivals Arsenal in the Fifth Round of the FA Cup.

'HALA MADRID' – 2003-04

Beckham and the Bernabeu Stadium seemed made for one another and Real's fans went wild when welcoming England's most celebrated player. The excitement and adulation continued when the team embarked a summer tour of the Far East, on which he was the star attraction.

When the serious business of the La Liga campaign began, David settled well into Real's midfield and really looked the part when strutting his stuff amid a stable of world-class talents.

He netted his first Spanish League goal within the first three minutes of an opening-day win against Real Betis at the Bernabeu. It was a great start for the club and for its newest recruit.

The campaign continued with Real Madrid defending their title and chasing a 30th La Liga success. But it wasn't to be – in the end Valencia wrapped up the title (their seventh) with Barcelona as runners-up ahead of La Coruna. Real finished a disappointing fourth. They were also knocked out in the European Champions' League quarter-finals, by Monaco.

Throughout 2003-04 David led England through the last of the European Championship qualifiers. In the hostile atmosphere of Skopje, Macedonia, he netted the winner from the penalty spot. He played against Liechtenstein at

According to reports, a football boot flew across the room during the post-match analysis and cut David's head.

The team pulled itself together after that and went on to achieve yet another Premier League title. They also reached the quarter-finals of the European Champions' League in which they were beaten by Real Madrid (the Spanish giants were soon to play a great part in David Beckham's future).

On the international front he led the England team into the Qualifying Group 7 campaign for the 2004 European Championship finals in Portugal. Beckham goals against Slovakia, Macedonia and Liechtenstein preceded the team's meeting with Turkey in Sunderland on 2 April 2003. David put in an inspired performance in the match and England eventually emerged as winners, with his last-minute penalty rounding off the scoreline at 2-0.

As the season drew to a close, and despite their worst fears, Manchester United fans everywhere had to accept the fact that their hero was going to leave Old Trafford. The dreaded rumours became reality on 2 July 2003, when David signed for reigning Spanish champions Real Madrid in a £25 million transfer deal.

Old Trafford, another win – and in the all-important last Group 7 tie against Turkey in Istanbul on 11 October.

In order to finish top and avoid the play-offs England required a single point from that game. Faced with warnings of potential disorder among rival fans the FA had declined to sell tickets for the match, which meant there were no England fans present in the stadium.

But the hostile atmosphere generated by the Turkish fans did little to distract the Three Lions from the job in hand. They came for a point – and they got it, by keeping a blank score-sheet.

England might have had a full quota of points from the game if David hadn't missed a penalty, but that didn't matter in the end. The team had won through to the European Championship finals.

In Portugal the Three Lions were in First Round Group B along with Switzerland, Croatia and France their first and toughest opponents. Frank Lampard headed the opening goal on 38th minutes and the Three Lions would have gone further ahead if David had converted a 72nd minute penalty – but his spot-kick was brilliantly saved by Fabien Bartez. A valuable save for France; a costly one for England.

Deep in injury-time David's Real Madrid club mate Zinedine Zidane beat David James with a superb free-kick for 1-1. Then, with just seconds to go, a poor back-pass from Steven Gerrard left James stranded in no-man's-land with Thierry Henry bearing down on him. The 'keeper brought the striker down – and Zidane netted the winner for France from the resulting spot-kick.

Things improved for England in the next match, against Switzerland. Young Wayne Rooney was the star of the show with two goals in a 3-0 victory. After Wayne's first goal went on 23 minutes, David and the rest of the team leapt on him in celebration and sheer relief!

The win against the Swiss meant England went confidently into their last group game against Croatia. Rooney was again the star, scoring twice, as the Three Lions romped to a 4-2 victory after going

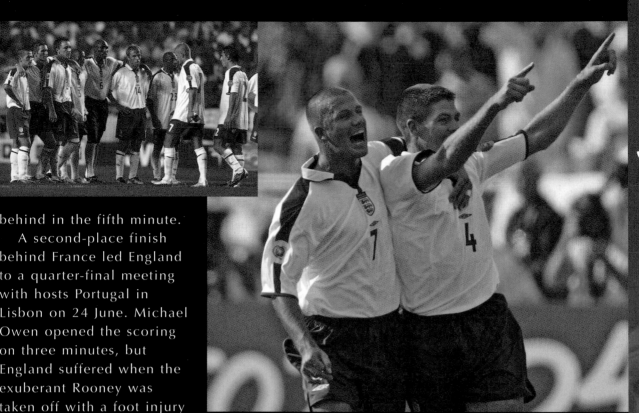

behind in the fifth minute.

A second-place finish behind France led England to a quarter-final meeting with hosts Portugal in Lisbon on 24 June. Michael Owen opened the scoring on three minutes, but England suffered when the exuberant Rooney was taken off with a foot injury after half-an-hour.

The thoroughly absorbing match went into extra-time with the scoreline at 1-1. Both sides scored in the added period and a penalty shoot-out came into play.

Against all the odds David skied the ball over the bar – an unbelievable error that was cancelled out when Rui Costa missed Portugal's third attempt. After that each kick went in until Ricardo saved Darius Vassell's effort. The Portuguese goalie then proceeded to rub salt into England's wounds by firing the winning penalty past James.

To be stopped short just two games from the title was a devastating blow for David and his team-mates. As the tournament carried on, they could only watch on with astonishment and admiration as Greece confounded all expectations by beating Portugal in the final.

ENGLAND IN THE 2004 EUROPEAN CHAMPIONSHIP

QUALIFYING GROUP 7 RESULTS
12.10.2002 Slovakia 1, ENGLAND 2
16.10.2002 ENGLAND 2, Macedonia 2
29.03.2003 Liechtenstein 0, ENGLAND 2
02.04.2003 ENGLAND 2, Turkey 0
11.06.2003 ENGLAND 2, Slovakia 0
06.09.2003 Macedonia 1, ENGLAND 2
10.09.2003 ENGLAND 2, Liechtenstein 0
11.10.2003 Turkey 0, ENGLAND 0

GROUP 7 FINAL TABLE
	P	W	D	L	F	A	Pts
ENGLAND	8	6	2	0	14	5	20
Turkey	8	6	1	1	17	5	19
Slovakia	8	3	1	4	11	9	10
Macedonia	8	1	3	4	11	14	6
Liechtenstein	8	0	1	7	2	22	1

FINALS TOURNAMENT GROUP B RESULTS
France 2, ENGLAND 1
ENGLAND 3, Switzerland 0
Croatia 2, ENGLAND 4

GROUP B TABLE
	P	W	D	L	F	A	Pts
France	3	2	0	1	7	4	7
ENGLAND	3	2	1	0	8	4	6
Croatia	3	0	1	2	4	6	6
Switzerland	3	0	2	1	1	6	1

QUARTER-FINALS
Portugal 2, ENGLAND 2 (Portugal won 6-5 on penalties)

Real Life (2004-05)

David's first appearance of the 2004-05 season was in England's colours in a Friendly encounter with Ukraine at Newcastle's St James' Park on 18 August 2004.

He opened the scoring in the 27th minute, with his first international goal in 11 appearances. The strike came at just the right time as England's defence had been enduring a torrid time at the hands of the lively Ukranian attackers.

The goal settled the home side and they gradually took control of the proceedings. Early in the second half, David set up his new Real Madrid team-mate Michael Owen who headed home England's second, and in the 72nd minute Shaun Wright-Phillips was on target to round

off the scoreline at 3-0.

David next appeared for England in the first 2006 World Cup Group Six qualifying games in Austria and Poland.

The first game in Vienna on 4 September ended in

a 2-2 draw, after England squandered a 2-0 lead in the last 19 minutes.

It was David's quick thinking that had led to England's first goal when, after a free-kick, he picked out the unmarked Frank Lampard who netted from close range in the 24th minute. Forty minutes later Steven Gerrard made it 2-0 with a 20-yard pile-driver.

It all went horribly wrong for England after that. Austria pulled one back with a curling free-kick for 2-1. Then David James fumbled a shot that went in under his body, and the points were shared.

Thankfully England's World Cup challenge got back on track when David led the team to a 2-1 win in Poland four days later, although the difference was made through a Polish own-goal.

At Real Madrid there was change of coach when Carlos Quieroz returned to Manchester United. He was succeeded as the Bernabeu's new boss by Jose Comacho who took over for a month in the summer before Mariano Garcia Remon jumped into the hot-seat ahead of the season's start. Remon lasted until the end of the year then he was replaced by Vanderlei Luxemburgo. Real's rocky mid-season spell is perhaps reflected in these managerial moves.

In addition to Michael Owen joining from Liverpool, Real's playing staff was boosted in 2004-05 by two other players from the English Premier League – Newcastle's polished centre-half Jonathan Woodgate and Danish star Thomas Gravesen from Everton. Gravesen arrived in January to bolster the midfield.

David embarked on his second Real Madrid season in a 1-0 defeat of Mallorca in the Spanish League. It was a great result for a club determined to better its fourth-place finish of 2003-04.

REAL MADRID'S ROLL OF HONOUR

Spanish League Champions (29 times): 1931-32, 1932-33, 1953-54, 1954-55, 1956-57, 1957-58, 1960-61, 1961-62, 1962-63, 1963-64, 1964-65, 1966-67, 1967-68, 1968-69, 1971-72, 1974-75, 1975-76, 1977-78, 1978-79, 1979-80, 1985-86, 1986-87, 1987-88, 1988-89, 1989-90, 1994-95, 1996-97, 2000-01, 2002-03

Spanish Cup Winners (17 times): 1905, 1906, 1907, 1908, 1917, 1934, 1936, 1946, 1947, 1962, 1970, 1974, 1975, 1980, 1982, 1989, 1993

European Cup Winners (nine times): 1956, 1957, 1958, 1959, 1960, 1966, 1998, 2000, 2002

UEFA Cup Winners (twice): 1985, 1986

World Club Cup Winners (three times): 1960, 1998, 2002

That particular campaign simply hadn't been good enough for one of the world's most prestigious footballing outfits. The legions of 'Los Galacticos' fans are accustomed to success on an enormous scale. After all, their team has worn the European Champions crown more often than any other (nine times) and has lifted the Spanish national title on 29 occasions – almost twice as often as their closest rivals, Barcelona.

Just as they had done many times in the past it was Barcelona, now managed by former Dutch star Frank Rijkaard, who provided the biggest obstacle to Real's latest La Liga ambitions. When the two teams met for the first 'El Classico' derby game of the 2004-05 season in the magnificent Nou Camp Stadium in November, it was Barca who had the edge. And on their home patch they demonstrated exactly why they were favourites for the title with a 3-0 victory over the white-shirted-ones.

That result came a few days after David had led England in a friendly international against Spain at the Bernabeu. Spain won thanks to a single Del Horno goal, but the whole occasion was seriously marred by some unsavoury and disgraceful behaviour from certain sections of the home crowd.

When Barcelona visited Madrid as table-toppers in mid-April, the La Liga picture was far clearer. Now Real really had to do well against their rivals if they were to stay in with a chance of winning the title.

The match proved to be a top-notch 'classico', a thoroughly absorbing and exciting encounter full of fine football – especially from the home team. David was the star of the show, making telling pass after telling pass, generally ruling the roost and collecting the Man of the Match plaudits.

Real won 4-2, with Michael Owen's strike the best of the bunch. It was a goal 'Made in England' with David's defence-

splitting ball opening the door for Michael to score. The stirring victory meant Real lived to fight another day and were still within catching distance of Barcelona.

On 1 May, the day before David's 30th

birthday, he set up one of Ronaldo's two goals in a 2-0 victory at Real Sociedad. The result trimmed Barca's lead to just three points.

In the end, though, time ran out for Real. As they were drawing 2-2 at Sevilla

SPANISH PRIMERA LEAGUE TABLE 2004-05

	P	W	D	L	F	A	Pts
Barcelona	38	25	9	4	73	29	84
REAL MADRID	38	25	5	8	71	32	80
Villareal	38	18	11	9	69	37	65
Real Betis	38	16	14	8	62	50	62
Espanyol	38	17	10	11	54	46	61
Sevilla	38	17	9	12	44	41	60
Valencia	38	14	16	8	54	39	58
Athletic Bilbao	38	14	9	15	59	54	51
La Coruna	38	12	15	11	46	50	51
Malaga	38	15	6	17	40	48	51
Atletico Madrid	38	13	11	14	40	34	50
Real Zaragoza	38	14	8	16	52	57	50
Getafe	38	12	11	15	38	46	47
Real Sociedad	38	13	8	17	47	56	47
Osasuna	38	12	10	16	46	65	46
Santander	38	12	8	18	41	58	44
Mallorca	38	10	9	19	42	63	39
Levante	38	9	10	19	39	58	37
Numancia	38	6	11	21	30	61	29
Albacete	38	6	10	22	33	56	28

on 22 May, Barcelona were wrapping up their 17th La Liga title success in a 1-1 draw at Levante. David and his illustrious team-mates had to settle for the runners-up spot and the consolation of securing another tilt at the European Champions League in 2005-06.

The club had certainly not matched up to its Euro expectations in 2004-05 – Juventus knocked them out with a disappointing last-16 defeat. David played in six Euro encounters during the season.

Due to injuries within the squad David played in defence in the last but one fixture of the La Liga campaign, a 0-0 draw with Madrid rivals Atletico. He missed the last game of the campaign against Real Zaragoza on 29 May.

A few days later he was in Chicago, leading the Three Lions side against Colombia in the second of England's summer friendlies played in the USA.

The game was notable, of course for Michael Owen's sensational hat-trick in a 3-2 victory. Captain David almost got his name on the score-sheet too, but saw his shot scrambled away by Colombian 'keeper Mondragon.

England's third goal was 'Made in Madrid', with Becks supplying the cross from which his Bernabeu team-mate Owen volleyed home to complete a sublime performance.

Earlier in the season David had worn the skipper's armband in England's 0-0 Friendly draw with Holland at Villa Park in February, and more importantly in two more World Cup qualifying campaign victories. The first being a 4-0 win over Northern Ireland at Old Trafford on 26 March.

Four days later he netted England's second goal in a 2-0 victory against Azerbaijan in Newcastle, after Steven Gerrard had opened the scoring. These two results kept England on track for the 2006 finals in Germany.

Watch this space...

David's games for Real in 2004-05 appear in his Career Record starting on page 55.

Playmaker

David Beckham possesses all the skills required of a professional footballer. But perhaps his greatest asset is his ability to 'read' a game to perfection – something shared by all world-class players.

Watch him in action and you'll see that he is constantly assessing the situation. He seems aware of all that's going on around him. He generally knows where his team-mates are while keeping a watchful eye on the movement of the opposition.

Note that he also knows – instinctively – what he intends to do with the ball before he receives it and more often than not he follows-up with a positive, constructive action.

Getting-A-Head!

Throughout his seasons in the spotlight, David's hairstyles have had almost as much attention as his skills on the football pitch...

The Set Piece Prince

Nobody Bends it like Beckham...

Whenever the referee blows his whistle to award a foul to England or Real Madrid – be it for a direct or indirect free-kick, a corner or a penalty, David Beckham is the man who invariably steps up to take it.

And there's a very good reason for this – he is an expert in any dead-ball situation.

Sometimes the ball doesn't go exactly where he intended it to go, but such occasions are rare indeed.

More often than not he will find his target from whatever range. It might be the head of an incoming attacker, the swift moving feet of a team-mate – or the back of the opponents' goal net.

David has acquired these deadly skills through years and years of dedication and training. He was, of course, blessed with natural talent as a youngster, but it was all that practice that gives him the edge.

The sure-footed Beckham can be relied upon to produce the most accurate dead-ball kicks in the game!

Captain Cool

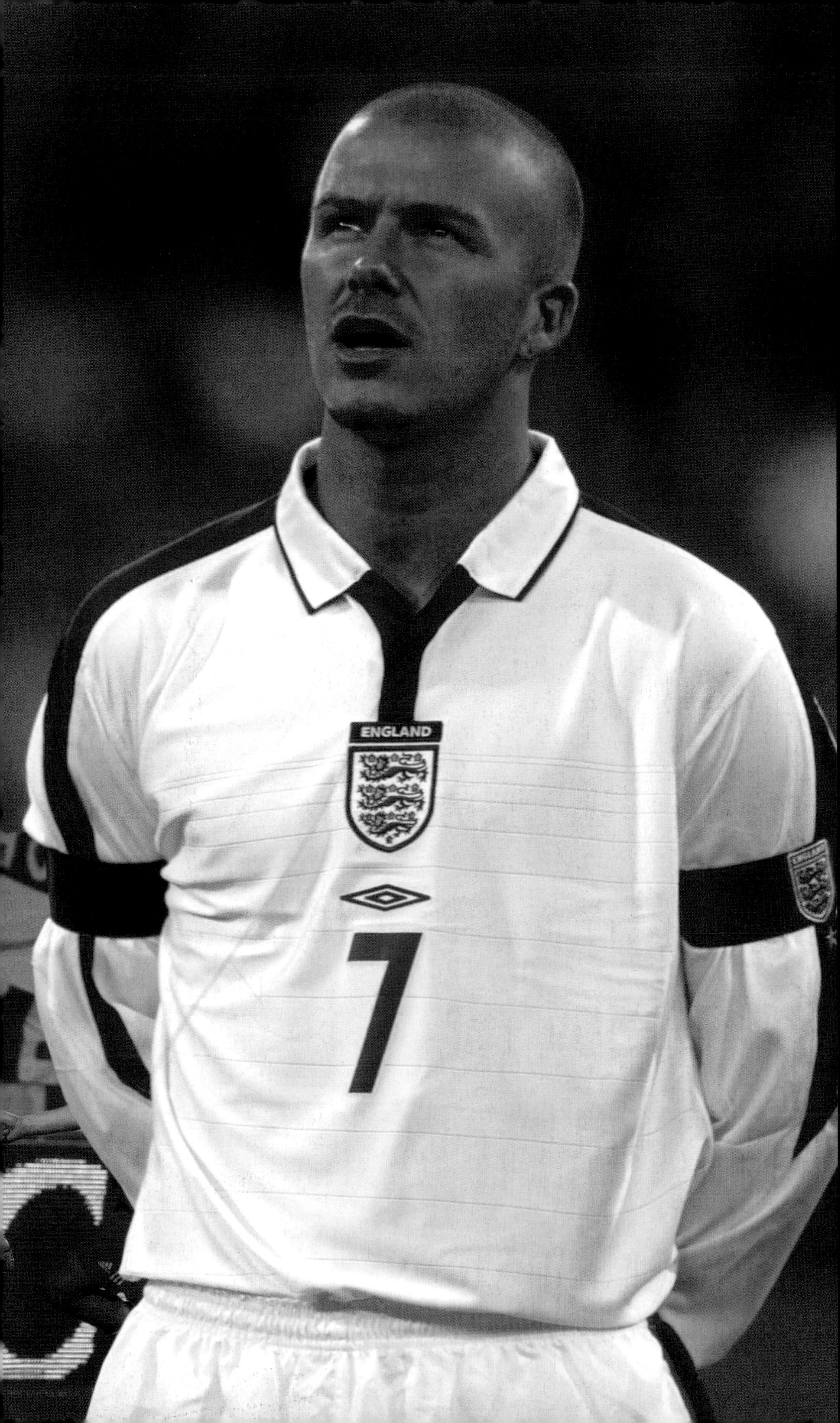

Posh & Becks

Like most red-blooded young males in Britain in 1997, David Beckham was a fan of the Spice Girls. In particular he fancied the slim, dark-haired one known as 'Posh Spice' and even confessed as much to his good friend and team-mate, Gary Neville.

On 22 February '97 David lined-up for Manchester United against Chelsea in a Premier League match at Stamford Bridge in south-west London. Watching from the East Stand were two of the Spice Girls – Melanie Chisholm aka 'Sporty Spice' and Victoria Adams, none other than 'Posh Spice' herself.

Victoria had no particular interest in soccer and had been brought along for her footballing baptism by Liverpool fanatic Mel C. Along with more than 28,000 others they saw David volley

home United's equaliser in an absorbing 1-1 draw.

After the game the two pop stars mingled with the players for a while in Chelsea's hospitality suite – yet somehow David and Victoria did not meet on that occasion.

Gutted that he had missed the opportunity of meeting the girl of his dreams, David made a few phone calls and discovered that Victoria was scheduled to be at a certain London location during the next few days. But when he got there, she was nowhere to be seen.

On 15 March 1997, almost a month after the match at Stamford Bridge, David played for Manchester United against Sheffield Wednesday at Old Trafford.

By interval time United were leading 1-0. While the players rested in the dressing room the fans

were being informed that Posh and Sporty Spice were about to draw a touch-line raffle. As the appreciative roar of the crowd penetrated through to the dressing room, the news that two of the Spice Girls were at the match reached the players. David excitedly asked 'Which ones?' but no one was sure.

After they'd drawn the raffle, a local radio journalist interviewed the two Spice Girls. When he asked Victoria to name her favourite player she leaned toward his microphone: 'David Beckham is very good,' she said, putting him first on her list, before adding Ryan Giggs and Eric Cantona to it.

In the second period, United scored again and secured three more valuable points to add to their Premiership challenge. After the match David spotted Victoria chatting with Mel C and other guests in the players' lounge. This time he made sure that he introduced himself to the 'Posh' one.

Victoria Caroline Adams was one of the five most recognisable young women in the world, with a public profile even higher than David's was at the time. As a member of the mega successful Spice Girls she was constantly in the public eye.

Together with her four band-mates, Victoria had

enjoyed astonishing success since the quintet's first record 'Wannabe' was released in the summer of 1996.

Raised in comfortable surroundings by Mum Jackie and Dad Tony in Cheshunt, Herts, she was the eldest of the three Adams children; she had a sister and a brother. Perhaps inheriting her love of show business from Dad, who had once played in a band called The Sonics, Victoria was stage struck from an early age.

She first stepped into the spotlight in the leading role in a school production of The Pied Piper. That was just the start for a girl driven by an unwavering ambition. She attended countless auditions as a teenager and refused to be put off if she didn't get the role she was chasing. She simply went on trying.

She enrolled at a Surrey stage academy after leaving school and followed that with a job in a touring theatre company specialising in musical productions.

Her Big Break came right out of the blue after spotting an advertisement in The Stage newspaper: 'RU 18-23 with the ability to sing/dance, streetwise, outgoing, ambitious and dedicated?'

Victoria ticked all the boxes – and quickly dashed-off her reply.

The letter led to an open audition in London along with the 400 or so others who had also answered the ad. Like everyone else, young Ms Adams was given less than a minute to Wow! the two impresarios determined to form an all-girl group to rival the boy bands that were enjoying such incredible success at the time.

Victoria made it to the last ten, from among whom the brand new band members would be selected. Following another round of auditions she found herself in the final five along with Melanie Brown, Melanie Chisholm and Michelle Stevenson. The fifth member – Geri Halliwell – was working on a Turkish TV game show and would join the group a few weeks later. Initially they were called 'Touch', but the name was soon changed to 'Spice'.

Sadly, Michelle had to leave the group for family reasons. She was replaced in the line-up by a pretty, blonde ex-child-model called Emma Bunton.

After many serious and intensive practice sessions at a recording studio in Surrey the group, renamed 'The Spice Girls', were ready to launch themselves onto the pop scene. They parted company with their original managers and signed on with Simon Fuller's 19 Management.

Under his astute guidance they soon tied up a recording deal which quickly led to the release of 'Wannabe'. The record and its video were launched in a flurry of publicity and Spice Girls' catchphrases like "Girl Power" and "Zig-A-Zig-Ah" quickly caught on.

The single shot straight to the UK's No. 1 spot, selling more than a million copies – and the Spice Girls were on their way to becoming the most famous band on Earth.

The release of 'Say You'll Be There' quickly followed and became the band's second Number One. Suddenly they were everywhere. Throughout the following months it seemed they were never off our TV screens and hardly a day went by without a Spice Girls headline appearing somewhere in the popular press.

They switched on the 1996 Christmas lights in London's Oxford Street. They hosted the Christmas Day edition of Top of the Pops. They released the phenomenally successful

Spice album. And before the year was out the release of '2Become1' gave them a permanent place in pop music history – as the first female group to have its first three singles hit the UK's top spot.

There was even more success for the Spice Girls in January 1997 when 'Wannabe' entered the US charts for the first time. The single continued its irresistible rise throughout February and on Saturday the 22nd it hit America's top spot. That was the day when Victoria went to Stamford Bridge with Mel C to see Chelsea play Manchester United...

After their eventual meeting at Old Trafford, David and Victoria quickly became a couple, and despite all efforts to keep their relationship secret it soon became public knowledge.

The romance between the soccer idol and the chart-topping pop star was, of course, a story made in tabloid heaven. Wherever they went, they found themselves dogged by the prying lenses of those ever-present snappers.

After a while the couple decided to have a bit of fun at the expense of the media. When Manchester United met Coventry at Old Trafford in August 1997, Victoria sat in the grandstand wearing an engagement ring. When the sharp-eyed press caught sight of it, the story broke that the couple were engaged at last. But the reports weren't true – Posh had worn the ring just for a laugh!

Their hectic schedules took them away from one another but they kept in close contact by phone. The question of marriage reportedly cropped up during one transatlantic call when Victoria was in the USA, on tour.

Their real engagement was announced in January 1998, around five months after the press had grasped the wrong-end-of-the-stick. This time David and Victoria were taking a well-earned break at an exclusive hotel in Cheshire, and the engagement rings proudly displayed for the press were 100% the real thing.

Needless to say, Victoria's band-mates and David's Man United team-mates were delighted – everyone was looking forward to the most talked about wedding of the '90s.

After a great deal of planning, the Big Day took place in July 1999. It was an elaborate ceremony at an enchanting castle in Ireland, with bride and groom occupying matching thrones! Now David and Victoria were Mr & Mrs.

Spot the Differences

At first glance these two pictures of David look alike – but someone has been tampering with them. Can you find 8 differences between them?

Solution appears on page 61

Name the Players

Can you recognise these images of some of David's present or former team-mates?

A

B

Teddy Sherigham

steven Gerad

C

Jony terry

D

luis figo

E

ser dinnars

Solution appears on page 61

Goal Ace

As a midfielder David Beckham's primary role is to create opportunities and openings for his team-mates. That's what he's best at. That's what he's paid for.

But, as we all know, he is certainly no slouch when presented with a goalscoring opportunity of his own. In fact, David has scored some of the most spectacular goals in recent football history...some vital ones too!

Who can forget his now legendary 'Halfway-Line' strike for Manchester United against Wimbledon on the first day of the 1997-98 season? And what about his stunning equaliser against Greece at Old Trafford in October 2001 - the goal that took England to the finals?

Here are some great shots of football's Golden Boy Going for Goal...

David's goals are listed in his Career Record starting on page 55.

40

Practice Makes Perfect

Here are some great shots of David in training...

Icon...
Inspiration...
Superstar...

David is a worldwide superstar, a sporting celebrity known in every football-playing country on Earth (and probably a few more besides)...

ROLE MODEL

As a sporting icon David is a positive role model for millions of youngsters all over the world. One magazine poll even placed him above Elvis Presley and Martin Luther King in terms of 'influence'. Wannabe footballers yearn to play the game the way he does. Women everywhere fancy him; grown men want to be like him and even those who can't stand soccer, recognise his status and his achievements.

MALE MODEL

If he hadn't become a football star, David could probably have made a pretty good living as a male model. As it is, he has probably appeared before as many camera lenses as any supermodel has!

FASHION LEADER

David looks good in whichever clothes he chooses to wear. He has appeared on numerous 'Best Dressed' lists throughout the years, usually at or near the top. He's something of a 'chameleon' too – can you think of any other modern celebrity who has changed his appearance quite so often?

AN ADVERTISER'S DREAM

David has endorsed numerous products over the years, including hair-care products, mobile phones, sunglasses, razors, computer games, soft drinks, menswear and sportswear. A huge proportion of his earnings comes from this area of his life.

MEETING 'N' GREETING

David has met many, many people on his travels, from his army of fans to some of the most famous figures in the world – including Nelson Mandela, Muhammad Ali, Tony Blair and Queen Elizabeth II (Her Majesty presented him with the OBE in 2003). Everyone agrees that he's a marvellous ambassador for the game of football and for the England team in particular. In this respect he has been compared to ex-Manchester United and England star Sir Bobby Charlton.

STATUE DAVID?

A gold leaf statue of David resides at a Buddhist temple in Thailand. It was made in 2000 and now stands proudly amongst similar effigies of other historical icons.

FOLLOWING IN DAVID'S FOOTSTEPS

The 'David Beckham Trail' was launched by the Waltham Forest Council in Spring 2005. This tourist attraction steers visitors around the landmarks of the great player's childhood and youth. Starting at David's birthplace – Whipps Cross Hospital in Leytonstone – the Trail takes in the schools, clubs and parks where his footballing prowess was first developed. This journey in Junior Beckham's footsteps takes around two hours and concludes at Chingford's Gilwell Park where the future footballer used to go camping when he was a member of the local Cub Scout troup.

KING OF BLING!

Jewellers love David – and David loves his jewellery. For instance, he reportedly owns a watch worth £50,000! It's encrusted with diamonds and matches his diamond and gold wedding band. Among other valuable pieces in his collection are a fabulous cross and diamond earrings.

FLASH! BANG! WALLOP!

If David and Victoria venture out to one of Madrid's trendy hot spots... If they fancy a quite meal in a little bistro somewhere... If they indulge a spot of retail therapy (and they do like nipping down to the shops every now and then)... If they decide to visit friends and family in the dear old UK... Well, wherever they go, they are usually trailed by a gaggle of pushy photographers, eager to capture the most trivial of snaps. Images of the celebrity couple sell for huge sums and hardly a week goes by without the appearance of one story or another about the Beckhams.

La Liga Wordsearch

Can you find the 15 Spanish teams in the grid below? They all played in La Liga in 2004-05. They may appear forwards, backwards or diagonally.

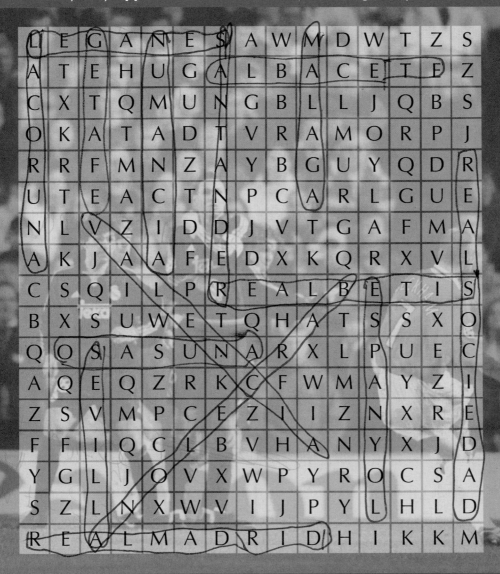

```
L E G A N E S A W M D W T Z S
A T E H U G A L B A C E T E Z
C X T Q M U N G B L L J Q B S
O K A T A D T V R A M O R P J
R R F M N Z A Y B G U Y Q D R
U T E A C T N P C A R L G U E
N L V Z I D D J V T G A F M A
A K J A A F E D X K Q R X V L
C S Q I L P R E A L B E T I S
B X S U W E T Q H A T S S X O
Q O S A S U N A R X L P U E C
A Q E Q Z R K C F W M A Y Z I
Z S V M P C E Z I I Z N X R E
F F I Q C L B V H A N Y X J D
Y G L J O V X W P Y R O C S A
S Z L N X W V I J P Y L H L D
R E A L M A D R I D H I K K M
```

Here are the teams you are searching for...

ALBACETE
BARCELONA
ESPANYOL
GETAFE
LA CORUNA
LEGANES
MALAGA
NUMANCIA

OSASUNA
REAL BETIS
REAL MADRID
REAL SOCIEDAD
SANTANDER
SEVILLA
VALENCIA

Solution appears on page 61

47

DB Quiz

Twenty tough questions to test your knowledge of England's skipper...

Johnathan ♡

1. How many English Premier League championship medals does David have? *6*
2. What is Real Madrid's nickname? *LOS galatics*
3. Where will the 2006 World Cup Finals take place? *In german*
4. In which year did David collect his FA Youth Cup winners medal? *1992*
5. What is David's astrological starsign? *Tayras*
6. Against which team did David make his Premier League debug? *Leed united*
7. In which year did David collect a European Champions' League winners' medal? *1ac*
8. In which country did Posh & Becks get married? *Ireland*
9. Which goalkeeper was on the receiving end of David's 'wonder goal' in 1996? *Nol*
10. Which country eliminated England from the Euro 2004 Championship? *Porugs win winoled*
11. In which English town was Victoria born? *Chesnan her desorashire*
12. Which English player joined Real Madrid from Newcastle in 2004? *Johnatho mod*
13. What is David's middle name? *Joseph*
14. Which birthday did David celebrate in May 2005? *his 30th*
15. Which English player joined Real Madrid from Liverpool in 2004?
16. Against which country did David first captain England?
17. What is Victoria's middle name?
18. With which club did David make his English League debut?
19. Under which manager did David make his English league debut?
20. What do the press call Posh & Becks' English mansion?

DB X-Word

Fourteen clues to solve…

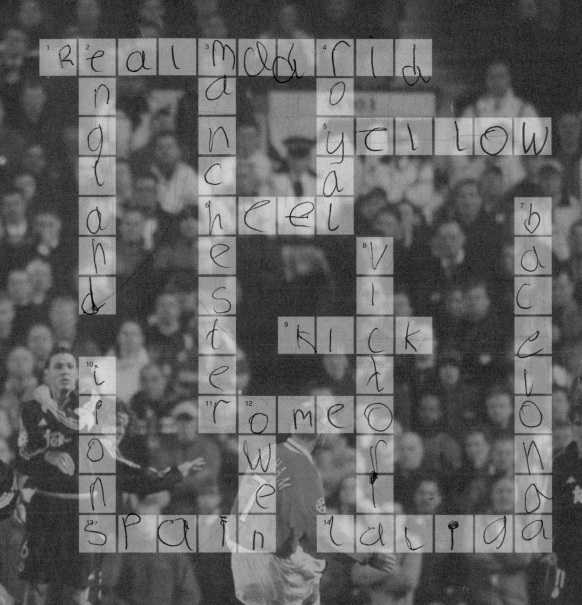

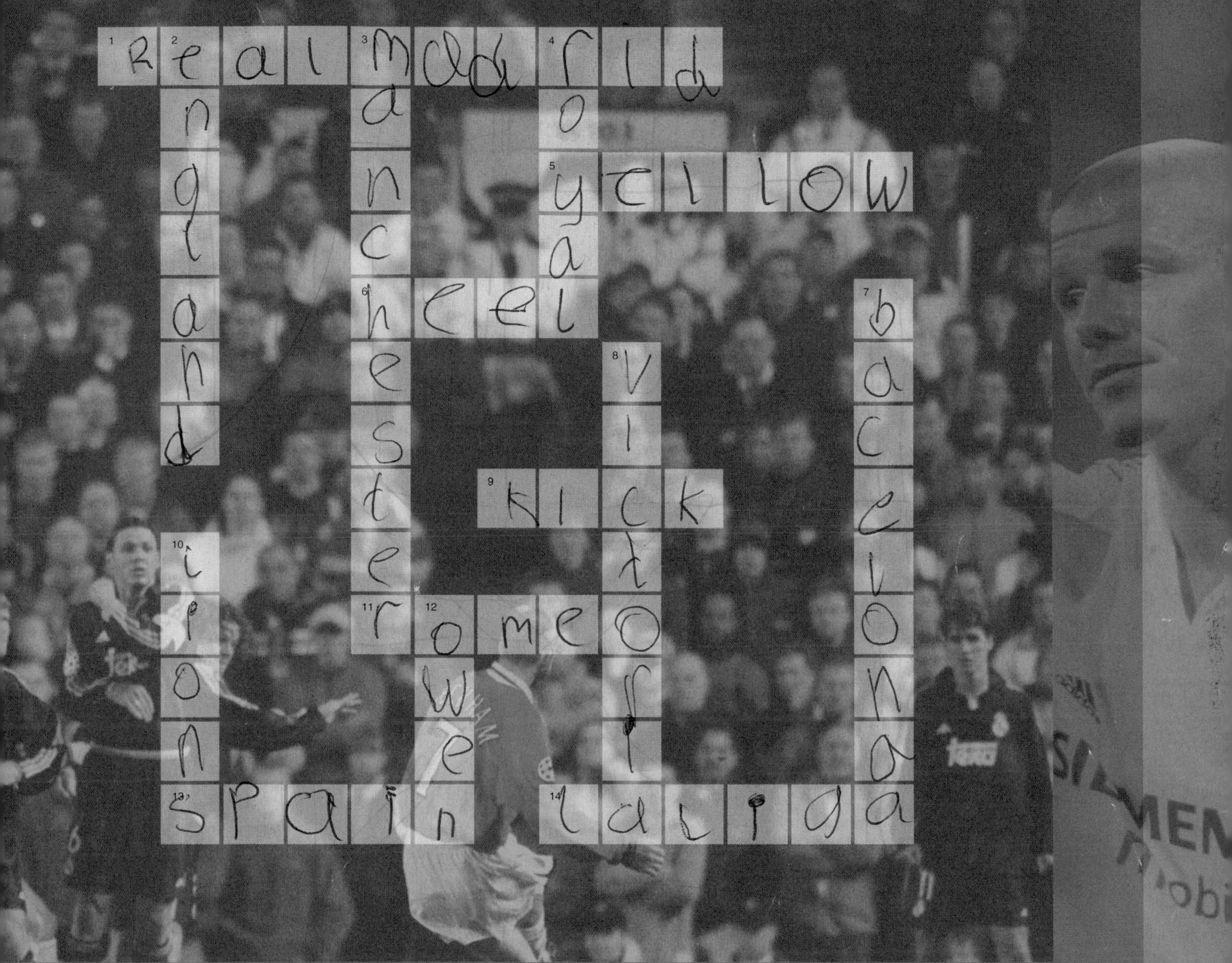

The completed crossword grid reads:

1 Across: REAL MADRID
2 Down: ENGLAND
3 Down: MANCHESTER
4 Down: ROYAL
5 Across: YELLOW
6 Across: HEEL
7 Down: BACELONA
8 Down: VICTORIA
9 Across: KICK
10 Down: ICONS
11 Across: ROMEO
12 Down: OWEN
13 Across: SPAIN
14 Across: LALIGA

ACROSS

1 David's club
5 Card colour
6 Part of foot
9 '____' the ball
11 David's second son
13 Country where David lives
14 Name of the Spanish League

DOWN

2 David's country
3 City where David became famous
4 English word for 'Real'
7 Real Madrid's greatest rivals
8 David's wife
10 Three '_____'; nickname for England
12 Michael _____, David's English club-mate

49

Family Man

On Sunday 20 February 2005, David and Victoria were absolutely delighted by the birth of their third son. He arrived in the world at Madrid's Hospital Ruber Internacional at

the unusual names given to their first two boys – five-year-old Brooklyn and two-year-old Romeo.

And, once again, the celebrity couple did not disappoint. They named the

waiting reporters that the baby had Victoria's nose and lips and he was "gorgeous". He later said he was "enjoying every moment of fatherhood for a third time".

Ever since the birth of Brooklyn in 1999 David and Victoria have shown themselves to be ideal parents. Let's check out a few snaps from the Beckham Family Album...

10.40 that morning.

The world's media waited with bated breath to learn what the Beckhams would call the little newcomer, especially after

baby Cruz, which is the Spanish word for 'cross'. David told the

David's Career Record

COMPETITIONS KEY
PL = Premier League
FL3 = Football League Div 3
FA = FA Cup
LC = League Cup
CS = Charity / Community Shield
EC = European Cup / European Champions'
    League
ESC = European Super Cup
WCC = World Club Championship
FCWC = FIFA Club World Championship
LL = La Liga
SSC = Spanish Super Cup
SC = Spanish Cup
FR = International Friendly
LT = Le Tournoi de France
ECQ = European Championship Qualifier
ECF = European Championship finals
WCQ = World Cup Qualifier
WCF = World Cup finals

SEASON 1992-93

Date	Comp	Opponents	Venue	Result	DB Goals
For MANCHESTER UNITED					
23.09.92	LC	Brighton & HA	A	D 1-1	-

SEASON 1994-95

Date	Comp	Opponents	Venue	Result	DB Goals
For MANCHESTER UNITED					
21.09.94	LC	Port Vale	A	W 2-1	-
05.10.94	LC	Port Vale	H	W 2-0	-
07.12.94	EC	Galatasary	H	W 4-0	1
28.01.95	FA	Wrexham	H	W 5-2	-
For PRESTON NORTH END (while on loan)					
04.03.95	FL3	Doncaster Rovers	H	D 2-2	1
11.03.95	FL3	Fulham	H	W 3-2	1
18.03.95	FL3	Bury	H	W 5-0	-
21.03.95	FL3	Exeter City	A	W 1-0	-
25.03.95	FL3	Lincoln City	A	D 1-1	-
For MANCHESTER UNITED					
02.04.95	PL	Leeds United	H	D 0-0	-
15.04.95	PL	Leicester City	A	W 4-0	-
17.04.95	PL	Chelsea	H	D 0-0	-
01.05.95	PL	Coventry City	A	W 3-2	-
For ENGLAND UNDER-21					
06.06.95	TT	Brazil	N	L 0-2	-
08.06.95	TT	Malaysia	N	W 2-0	-
10.06.95	TT	Angola	N	W 1-0	-
12.06.95	TT	France	N	L 0-2	-

SEASON 1995-96

Date	Comp	Opponents	Venue	Result	DB Goals
For MANCHESTER UNITED					
19.08.95	PL	Aston Villa	A	L 1-3	1
23.08.95	PL	West Ham United	H	W 2-1	-
26.08.95	PL	Wimbledon	H	W 3-1	-
28.08.95	PL	Blackburn Rovers	A	W 2-1	1
For ENGLAND UNDER-21					
02.09.95	FR	Portugal	A	L 0-2	-
For MANCHESTER UNITED					
09.09.95	PL	Everton	A	W 3-2	-
16.09.95	PL	Bolton Wanderers	H	W 3-0	-
20.09.95	LC	York City	H	L 0-3	-
23.09.95	PL	Sheffield Wed	A	D 0-0	-
01.10.95	PL	Liverpool	H	D 2-2	-
03.10.95	LC	York City	A	W 3-1	-
14.10.95	PL	Manchester City	H	W 1-0	-
04.11.95	PL	Arsenal	A	L 0-1	-
For ENGLAND UNDER-21					
14.11.95	FR	Austria	H	W 2-1	-
For MANCHESTER UNITED					
18.11.95	PL	Southampton	H	W 4-1	-
22.11.95	PL	Coventry City	A	W 4-0	1
27.11.95	PL	Nottingham Forest	A	D 1-1	-
02.12.95	PL	Chelsea	H	D 1-1	1
09.12.95	PL	Sheffield Wed	H	D 2-2	-
17.12.95	PL	Liverpool	A	L 0-2	-
24.12.95	PL	Leeds United	A	L 1-3	-
27.12.95	PL	Newcastle United	H	W 2-0	-
30.12.95	PL	QPR	H	W 2-1	-
01.01.96	PL	Tottenham H	A	L 1-4	-
06.01.96	FA	Sunderland	H	D 2-2	-
22.01.96	PL	West Ham United	A	W 1-0	-
03.02.96	PL	Wimbledon	A	W 4-2	-
10.02.96	PL	Blackburn Rovers	H	W 1-0	-
21.02.96	PL	Everton	H	W 2-0	-
25.02.96	PL	Bolton Wanderers	A	W 6-0	1
16.03.96	PL	QPR	A	D 1-1	-
24.03.96	PL	Tottenham H	H	W 1-0	-
31.03.96	FA	Chelsea	N	W 2-1	1
06.04.96	PL	Manchester City	A	W 3-2	-
08.04.96	PL	Coventry City	H	W 1-0	-
13.04.96	PL	Southampton	A	L 1-3	-
17.04.96	PL	Leeds United	H	W 1-0	-
28.04.96	PL	Nottingham Forest	H	W 5-0	2
05.05.96	PL	Middlesbrough	A	W 3-0	-
11.05.96	FA	Liverpool	N	W 1-0	-
For ENGLAND UNDER-21					
24.05.96	TT	Belgium	N	W 1-0	-
28.05.96	TT	Angola	N	L 0-2	-
30.05.96	TT	Portugal	N	L 1-3	-

7

SEASON 1996-97

Date	Comp	Opponents	Venue	Result	Goals
For MANCHESTER UNITED					
11.08.96	CS	Newcastle United	N	W 4-0	1
17.08.96	PL	Wimbledon	A	W 3-0	1
21.08.96	PL	Everton	H	D 2-2	-
25.08.96	PL	Blackburn Rovers	H	D 2-2	-
For ENGLAND					
01.09.96	WCQ	Moldova	A	W 3-0	-
For MANCHESTER UNITED					
04.09.96	PL	Derby County	A	D 1-1	1
07.09.96	PL	Leeds United	A	W 4-0	-
11.09.96	EC	Juventus	A	L 0-1	-
14.09.96	PL	Nottingham Forest	H	W 4-1	-
21.09.96	PL	Aston Villa	A	D 0-0	-
25.09.96	EC	Rapid Vienna	H	W 2-0	1
29.09.96	PL	Tottenham H	H	W 2-0	-
For ENGLAND					
09.10.96	WCQ	Poland	H	W 2-1	-
For MANCHESTER UNITED					
12.10.96	PL	Liverpool	H	W 1-0	1
16.10.96	EC	Fenerbahce	A	W 2-0	1
20.10.96	PL	Newcastle United	A	L 0-5	-
26.10.96	PL	Southampton	A	L 3-6	1
30.10.96	EC	Fenerbahce	H	L 0-1	-
02.11.96	PL	Chelsea	H	L 1-2	-
For ENGLAND					
09.11.96	WCQ	Georgia	A	W 2-0	-
For MANCHESTER UNITED					
16.11.96	PL	Arsenal	H	W 1-0	-
20.11.96	EC	Juventus	H	L 0-1	-
23.11.96	PL	Middlesbrough	A	D 2-2	-
30.11.96	PL	Leicester C	H	W 3-1	-
04.12.96	EC	Rapid Vienna	A	W 2-0	-
08.12.96	PL	West Ham Utd	A	D 2-2	1
18.12.96	PL	Sheffield Wed	A	D 1-1	-
26.12.96	PL	Nottingham F	A	W 4-0	1
28.12.96	PL	Leeds United	H	W 1-0	-
01.01.97	PL	Aston Villa	H	D 0-0	-
05.01.97	FA	Tottenham H	A	W 2-0	1
12.01.97	PL	Tottenham H	H	W 2-1	1
29.01.97	PL	Wimbledon	H	W 2-1	-
01.02.97	PL	Southampton	H	W 2-1	-
04.02.97	FA	Wimbledon	A	L 0-1	-
For ENGLAND					
12.02.97	WCQ	Italy	H	L 0-1	-
For MANCHESTER UNITED					
19.02.97	PL	Arsenal	A	W 2-1	-
22.02.97	PL	Chelsea	A	D 1-1	1
01.03.97	PL	Coventry City	H	W 3-1	-
05.03.97	EC	Porto	H	W 4-0	-
08.03.97	PL	Sunderland	A	L 1-2	-
15.03.97	PL	Sheffield Wed	H	W 2-0	-
19.03.97	EC	Porto	A	D 0-0	-
22.03.97	PL	Everton	A	L 0-2	-
05.04.97	PL	Derby County	A	L 2-3	-
09.04.97	EC	Bor Dortmund	A	L 0-1	-
12.04.97	PL	Blackburn Rovers	A	W 3-2	-
19.04.97	PL	Liverpool	A	W 3-1	-
23.04.97	EC	Bor Dortmund	H	L 0-1	-
For ENGLAND					
30.04.97	WCQ	Georgia	H	W 2-0	-
For MANCHESTER UNITED					
03.05.97	PL	Leicester City	A	D 2-2	-
05.05.97	PL	Middlesbrough	H	D 3-3	-
08.05.97	PL	Newcastle Utd	H	D 0-0	-
11.05.97	PL	West Ham Utd	H	W 2-0	-
For ENGLAND					
24.05.97	FR	South Africa	H	W 2-1	-
31.05.97	WCQ	Poland	A	W 2-0	-
04.06.97	LT	Italy	N	W 2-0	-
07.06.97	LT	France	A	W 1-0	-

SEASON 1997-98

Date	Comp	Opponents	Venue	Result	On Goals
For MANCHESTER UNITED					
03.08.97	CS	Chelsea	N	D 1-1	-
10.08.97	PL	Tottenham H	A	W 2-0	-
13.08.97	PL	Southampton	H	W 1-0	1
23.08.97	PL	Leicester City	A	D 0-0	-
27.08.97	PL	Everton	A	W 2-0	1
30.08.97	PL	Coventry City	H	W 3-0	-
For ENGLAND					
10.09.97	WCQ	Moldova	H	W 4-0	-
For MANCHESTER UNITED					
13.09.97	PL	West Ham Utd	H	W 2-1	-
17.09.97	EC	Kosice	A	W 3-0	-
20.09.97	PL	Bolton W	A	D 0-0	-
24.09.97	PL	Chelsea	H	D 2-2	-
27.09.97	PL	Leeds United	A	L 0-1	-
01.10.97	EC	Juventus	H	W 3-2	-
04.10.97	PL	Crystal Palace	H	W 2-0	-
For ENGLAND					
11.10.97	WCQ	Italy	A	D 0-0	-
For MANCHESTER UNITED					
18.10.97	PL	Derby County	A	D 2-2	-
22.10.97	EC	Feyenoord	H	W 2-1	-
25.10.97	PL	Barnsley	H	W 7-0	-
01.11.97	PL	Sheffield Wed	H	W 6-1	-
05.11.97	EC	Feyenoord	A	W 3-1	-
09.11.97	PL	Arsenal	A	L 2-3	-
For ENGLAND					
15.11.97	FR	Cameroon	H	W 2-0	-
For MANCHESTER UNITED					
22.11.97	PL	Wimbledon	A	W 5-2	2
27.11.97	EC	Kosice	H	W 3-0	-
30.11.97	PL	Blackburn Rovers	H	W 4-0	-
06.12.97	PL	Liverpool	A	W 3-1	1
10.12.97	EC	Juventus	A	L 0-1	-
15.12.97	PL	Aston Villa	H	W 1-0	-
21.12.97	PL	Newcastle United	A	W 1-0	-
26.12.97	PL	Everton	H	W 2-0	-
28.12.97	PL	Coventry City	A	L 2-3	-
04.01.98	FA	Chelsea	A	W 5-3	2
10.01.98	PL	Tottenham H	H	W 2-0	-
19.01.98	PL	Southampton	A	L 0-1	-
24.01.98	FA	Walsall	H	W 5-1	-
31.01.98	PL	Leicester City	A	L 0-1	-
07.02.98	PL	Bolton Wanderers	H	D 1-1	-
15.02.98	FA	Barnsley	H	D 1-1	-
18.02.98	PL	Aston Villa	A	W 2-0	1
21.02.98	PL	Derby County	H	W 2-0	-
25.02.98	FA	Barnsley	A	L 2-3	-
28.02.98	PL	Chelsea	A	W 1-0	-
04.03.98	EC	Monaco	A	D 0-0	-
07.03.98	PL	Sheffield Wed	A	L 0-2	-
11.03.98	PL	West Ham United	A	D 1-1	-
14.03.98	PL	Arsenal	H	L 0-1	-
18.03.98	EC	Monaco	H	D 1-1	-
28.03.98	PL	Wimbledon	H	W 2-0	-
06.04.98	PL	Blackburn Rovers	A	W 3-1	1
10.04.98	PL	Liverpool	H	D 1-1	-
18.04.98	PL	Newcastle United	H	D 1-1	1
For ENGLAND					
22.04.98	FR	Portugal	H	W 3-0	-
For MANCHESTER UNITED					
27.04.98	PL	Crystal Palace	A	W 3-0	-
04.05.98	PL	Leeds United	H	W 3-0	1

Date	Comp	Opponents	Venue	Result	On Goals
For ENGLAND					
23.05.98	FR	Saudi Arabia	H	D 0-0	-
29.05.95	FR	Belgium	N	D 0-0	-
22.06.98	WCF	Romania	N	L 1-2	-
26.06.98	WCF	Colombia	N	W 2-0	1
30.06.98	WCF	Argentina	N	D 2-2*	-

(*Argentina won on penalties)

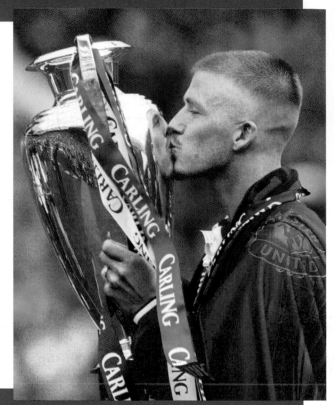

SEASON 1998-99

Date	Comp	Opponents	Venue	Result	On Goals
For MANCHESTER UNITED					
09.08.98	CS	Arsenal	N	L 0-3	-
12.08.98	EC	LKS Lodz	H	W 2-0	-
15.08.98	PL	Leicester City	H	D 2-2	1
22.08.98	PL	West Ham United	A	D 0-0	-
26.08.98	EC	LKS Lodz	A	D 0-0	-
09.09.98	PL	Charlton Athletic	H	W 4-1	-
12.09.98	PL	Coventry City	H	W 2-0	-
16.09.98	EC	Barcelona	H	D 3-3	1
20.09.98	PL	Arsenal	A	L 0-3	-
24.09.98	PL	Liverpool	H	W 2-0	-
30.09.98	EC	Bayern Munich	A	D 2-2	-
03.10.98	PL	Southampton	A	W 3-0	-
For ENGLAND					
14.10.98	ECQ	Luxembourg	A	W 3-0	-
For MANCHESTER UNITED					
17.10.98	PL	Wimbledon	H	W 5-1	1
24.10.98	PL	Derby County	A	D 1-1	-
31.10.98	PL	Everton	A	W 4-1	-
04.11.98	EC	Brondby	H	W 5-0	1
08.11.98	PL	Newcastle United	H	D 0-0	-
14.11.98	PL	Blackburn Rovers	A	W 3-2	-
For ENGLAND					
18.11.98	FR	Czech Republic	H	W 2-0	-
For MANCHESTER UNITED					
21.11.98	PL	Sheffield Wed	A	L 1-3	-
25.11.98	EC	Barcelona	A	D 3-3	-
01.12.98	LC	Tottenham H	A	L 1-3	-
05.12.98	PL	Aston Villa	A	D 1-1	-

Date	Comp	Opponents	Venue	Result	Goals
09.12.98	EC	Bayern Munich	A	D 1-1	-
12.12.98	PL	Tottenham H	A	D 2-2	-
16.12.98	PL	Chelsea	H	D 1-1	-
19.12.98	PL	Middlesbrough	H	L 2-3	-
26.12.98	PL	Nottingham Forest	H	W 3-0	-
29.12.98	PL	Chelsea	A	D 0-0	-
16.01.99	PL	Leicester City	A	W 6-2	-
24.01.99	FA	Liverpool	H	W 2-1	-
31.01.99	PL	Charlton Athletic	A	W 1-0	-
06.02.99	PL	Nottingham Forest	A	W 8-1	-

For ENGLAND

10.02.99	FR	France	H	L 0-2	-

For MANCHESTER UNITED

14.02.99	FA	Fulham	H	W 1-0	-
17.02.99	PL	Arsenal	H	D 1-1	-
20.02.99	PL	Coventry City	A	W 1-0	-
27.02.99	PL	Southampton	H	W 2-1	-
03.03.99	EC	Inter Milan	H	W 2-0	-
07.03.99	FA	Chelsea	H	D 0-0	-
10.03.99	FA	Chelsea	A	W 2-0	-
13.03.99	PL	Newcastle United	A	W 2-1	-
17.03.99	EC	Inter Milan	A	D 1-1	-
21.03.99	PL	Everton	H	W 3-1	1

For ENGLAND

27.03.99	ECQ	Poland	H	W 3-1	-

For MANCHESTER UNITED

03.04.99	PL	Wimbledon	A	D 1-1	1
07.04.99	EC	Juventus	H	D 1-1	-
11.04.99	FA	Arsenal	N	D 0-0	-
14.04.99	FA	Arsenal	N	W 2-1	1
21.04.99	EC	Juventus	A	W 3-2	-
25.04.99	PL	Leeds United	A	D 1-1	-
01.05.99	PL	Aston Villa	H	W 2-1	1
05.05.99	PL	Liverpool	A	D 2-2	-
09.05.99	PL	Middlesbrough	A	W 1-0	-
12.05.99	PL	Blackburn Rovers	A	D 0-0	-
16.05.99	PL	Tottenham H	H	W 2-1	1
22.05.99	FA	Newcastle United	N	W 2-0	-
26.05.99	EC	Bayern Munich	N	W 2-1	-

For ENGLAND

05.06.99	ECQ	Sweden	H	D 0-0	-

SEASON 1999-2000

Date	Comp	Opponents	Venue	Result	On Goal

For MANCHESTER UNITED

01.08.99	CS	Arsenal	N	L 1-2	1
08.08.99	PL	Everton	A	D 1-1	-
11.08.99	PL	Sheffield Wed	H	W 4-0	-
14.08.99	PL	Leeds United	H	W 2-0	-
22.08.99	PL	Arsenal	A	W 2-1	-
25.08.99	PL	Coventry City	A	W 2-1	-
27.08.99	ESC	Lazio	N	L 0-1	-
30.08.99	PL	Newcastle United	H	W 5-1	-

For ENGLAND

04.09.99	ECQ	Luxembourg	H	W 6-0	-
08.09.99	ECQ	Poland	A	D 0-0	-

For MANCHESTER UNITED

11.09.99	PL	Liverpool	A	W 3-2	-
14.09.99	EC	Dynamo Zagreb	H	D 0-0	-
22.09.99	EC	Sturm Graz	A	W 3-0	-
25.09.99	PL	Southampton	H	D 3-3	-
29.09.99	EC	Marseille	H	W 2-1	-
03.10.99	PL	Chelsea	A	L 0-5	-
16.10.99	PL	Watford	H	W 4-1	-
19.10.99	EC	Marseille	A	L 0-1	-
23.10.99	PL	Tottenham H	A	L 1-3	-
27.10.99	EC	Dynamo Zagreb	A	W 2-1	1
30.10.99	PL	Aston Villa	H	W 3-0	-

For ENGLAND

13.11.99	ECQ	Scotland	A	W 2-0	-
17.11.99	ECQ	Scotland	H	L 0-1	-

For MANCHESTER UNITED

20.11.99	PL	Derby County	A	W 2-1	-
23.11.99	EC	Fiorentina	A	L 0-2	-
30.11.99	WCC	Palmeiras	N	W 1-0	-
08.12.99	EC	Valencia	H	W 3-0	-
18.12.99	PL	West Ham United	A	W 4-2	-
28.12.99	PL	Sunderland	A	D 2-2	-
06.01.00	FCWC	Necaxa	A	D 1-1	-
11.01.00	FCWC	Sth Melbourne	A	W 2-0	-
24.01.00	PL	Arsenal	H	D 1-1	-
29.01.00	PL	Middlesbrough	H	W 1-0	1
02.02.00	PL	Sheffield Wed	A	W 1-0	-
05.02.00	PL	Coventry City	H	W 3-2	-
12.02.00	PL	Newcastle United	A	L 0-3	-

For ENGLAND

23.02.00	FR	Argentina	H	D 0-0	-

For MANCHESTER UNITED

26.02.00	PL	Wimbledon	A	D 2-2	-
01.03.00	EC	Bordeaux	H	W 2-0	-
04.03.00	PL	Liverpool	H	D 1-1	-
07.03.00	EC	Bordeaux	A	W 2-1	-
11.03.00	PL	Derby County	H	W 3-1	-
15.03.00	EC	Fiorentina	H	W 3-1	-
18.03.00	PL	Leicester City	A	W 2-0	1
25.03.00	PL	Bradford City	A	W 4-0	1
01.04.00	PL	West Ham Utd	H	W 7-1	1
04.04.00	EC	Real Madrid	A	D 0-0	-
10.04.00	PL	Middlesbrough	A	W 4-3	-
15.04.00	PL	Sunderland	H	W 4-0	-
19.04.00	EC	Real Madrid	H	L 2-3	1
22.04.00	PL	Southampton	A	W 3-1	1
24.04.00	PL	Chelsea	H	W 3-2	-
06.05.00	PL	Tottenham H	H	W 3-1	1

For ENGLAND

27.05.00	FR	Brazil	H	D 1-1	-
31.05.00	FR	Ukraine	H	W 2-0	-
03.06.00	FR	Malta	A	W 2-1	-
12.06.00	ECF	Portugal	N	L 2-3	-
17.06.00	ECF	Germany	N	W 1-0	-
20.06.00	ECF	Romania	N	L 2-3	-

SEASON 2000-01

Date	Comp	Opponents	Venue	Result	De Goals
For MANCHESTER UNITED					
13.08.00	CS	Chelsea	N	L 0-2	-
20.08.00	PL	Newcastle United	H	W 2-0	-
22.08.00	PL	Ipswich Town	A	D 1-1	1
26.08.00	PL	West Ham United	A	D 2-2	1
For ENGLAND					
02.09.00	FR	France	A	D 1-1	-
For MANCHESTER UNITED					
05.09.00	PL	Bradford City	H	W 6-0	1
09.09.00	PL	Sunderland	H	W 3-0	-
13.09.00	EC	Anderlecht	H	W 5-1	-
16.09.00	PL	Everton	A	W 3-1	-
19.09.00	EC	Dynamo Kiev	A	D 0-0	-
23.09.00	PL	Chelsea	A	D 3-3	1
26.09.00	EC	PSV Eindhoven	A	L 1-3	-
01.10.00	PL	Arsenal	A	L 0-1	-
For ENGLAND					
07.10.00	WCQ	Germany	H	L 0-1	-
For MANCHESTER UNITED					
18.10.00	EC	PSV Eindhoven	H	W 3-1	-
21.10.00	PL	Leeds United	H	W 3-0	1
24.10.00	EC	Anderlecht	A	L 1-2	-
28.10.00	PL	Southampton	H	W 5-0	-
04.11.00	PL	Coventry City	A	W 2-0	1
08.11.00	EC	Dynamo Kiev	H	W 1-0	-
11.11.00	PL	Middlesbrough	H	W 2-1	-
For ENGLAND					
15.11.00	FR	Italy	A	L 0-1	-
For MANCHESTER UNITED					
18.11.00	PL	Manchester City	A	W 1-0	1
21.11.00	EC	Panathiniakos	H	W 3-1	-
02.12.00	PL	Tottenham H	H	W 2-0	-
06.12.00	EC	Sturm Graz	A	W 2-0	-
09.12.00	PL	Charlton Athletic	A	D 3-3	-
17.12.00	PL	Liverpool	H	L 0-1	-
23.12.00	PL	Ipswich Town	H	W 2-0	-
26.12.00	PL	Aston Villa	A	W 1-0	-
30.12.00	PL	Newcastle United	A	D 1-1	1
01.01.01	PL	West Ham United	H	W 3-1	-
07.01.01	FA	Fulham	A	W 2-1	-
13.01.01	PL	Bradford City	A	W 3-0	-
28.01.01	FA	West Ham United	H	L 0-1	-
31.01.01	PL	Sunderland	A	W 1-0	-
03.02.01	PL	Everton	H	W 1-0	-
10.02.01	PL	Chelsea	A	D 1-1	-
14.02.01	EC	Valencia	A	D 0-0	-
20.02.01	EC	Valencia	H	D 1-1	-
25.02.01	PL	Arsenal	H	W 6-1	-
For ENGLAND					
28.02.01	FR	Spain	H	W 3-0	-
For MANCHESTER UNITED					
03.03.01	PL	Leeds United	A	D 1-1	-
07.03.01	EC	Panathiniakos	A	D 1-1	-
For ENGLAND					
24.03.01	WCQ	Finland	H	W 2-1	1
28.03.01	WCQ	Albania	A	W 3-1	-
For MANCHESTER UNITED					
31.03.01	PL	Liverpool	A	L 0-2	-
03.04.01	EC	Bayern Munich	H	L 0-1	-
14.04.01	PL	Coventry City	H	W 4-2	-
21.04.01	PL	Manchester City	H	D 1-1	-
28.04.01	PL	Middlesbrough	A	W 2-0	1
05.05.01	PL	Derby County	H	L 0-1	-

Date	Comp	Opponents	Venue	Result	De Goals
For ENGLAND					
25.05.01	FR	Mexico	H	W 4-0	1
06.06.01	WCQ	Greece	A	W 2-0	1

SEASON 2001-02

Date	Comp	Opponents	Venue	Result	De Goals
For MANCHESTER UNITED					
12.08.01	CS	Liverpool	N	L 1-2	-
For ENGLAND					
15.08.01	FR	Holland	H	L 0-2	-
For MANCHESTER UNITED					
19.08.01	PL	Fulham	H	W 3-2	1
22.08.01	PL	Blackburn Rovers	A	D 2-2	1
26.08.01	PL	Aston Villa	A	D 1-1	-
For ENGLAND					
01.09.01	WCQ	Germany	A	W 5-1	-
05.09.01	WCQ	Albania	H	W 2-0	-
For MANCHESTER UNITED					
08.09.01	PL	Everton	H	W 4-1	1
15.09.01	PL	Newcastle United	A	L 3-4	-
18.09.01	EC	Lille	H	W 1-0	1
25.09.01	EC	La Coruna	A	L 1-2	-
29.09.01	PL	Tottenham H	A	W 5-3	1
For ENGLAND					
06.10.01	WCQ	Greece	H	D 2-2	1
For MANCHESTER UNITED					
10.10.01	EC	Olympiakos	A	W 2-0	1
17.10.01	EC	La Coruna	H	L 2-3	-
23.10.01	EC	Olympiakos	H	W 3-0	-
27.10.01	PL	Leeds United	H	D 1-1	-
31.10.01	EC	Lille	A	D 1-1	-
04.11.01	PL	Liverpool	A	L 1-3	1
For ENGLAND					
10.11.01	FR	Sweden	H	D 1-1	1
For MANCHESTER UNITED					
17.11.01	PL	Leicester City	H	W 2-0	

56

20.11.01	EC	Bayern Munich	A	D 1-1	-
25.11.01	PL	Arsenal	A	L 1-3	=
01.12.01	PL	Chelsea	H	L 0-3	-
08.12.01	PL	West Ham United	H	L 0-1	-
22.12.01	PL	Southampton	H	W 6-1	-
26.12.01	PL	Everton	A	W 2-0	=
30.12.01	PL	Fulham	A	W 3-2	=
02.01.02	PL	Newcastle United	H	W 3-1	=
06.01.02	FA	Aston Villa	A	W 3-2	-
13.01.02	PL	Southampton	A	W 3-1	1
19.01.02	PL	Blackburn Rover	H	W 2-1	-
22.01.02	PL	Liverpool	H	L 0-1	-
29.01.02	PL	Bolton Wanderers	A	W 4-0	-
02.02.02	PL	Sunderland	H	W 4-1	1
10.02.02	PL	Charlton Athletic	A	W 2-0	=

For *ENGLAND*

13.02.02	FR	Holland	A	D 1-1	-

For *MANCHESTER UNITED*

20.02.02	EC	Nantes	A	D 1-1	-
23.02.02	PL	Aston Villa	H	W 1-0	-
26.02.02	EC	Nantes	H	W 5-1	1
03.03.02	PL	Derby County	A	D 2-2	-
06.03.02	PL	Tottenham H	H	W 4-0	2
13.03.02	EC	Bayern Munich	H	D 0-0	-
16.03.02	PL	West Ham United	A	W 5-2	2
19.03.02	EC	Boavista	A	W 3-0	1
23.03.02	PL	Middlesbrough	A	L 0-1	-

For *ENGLAND*

27.03.02	FR	Italy	H	L 1-2	-

For *MANCHESTER UNITED*

30.03.02	PL	Leeds United	A	W 4-3	=
02.04.02	EC	La Coruna	A	W 2-0	1
10.04.02	EC	La Coruna	H	W 3-2	-

For *ENGLAND*

02.06.02	WCF	Sweden	N	D 1-1	-
07.06.02	WCF	Argentina	N	W 1-0	1
12.06.02	WCF	Nigeria	N	D 0-0	-
15.06.02	WCF	Denmark	N	W 3-0	-
21.06.02	WCF	Brazil	N	L 1-2	

SEASON 2002-03
For *MANCHESTER UNITED*

14.08.02	EC	Zalaegerszeg	A	L 0-1	-
17.08.02	PL	West Brom	H	W 1-0	

23.08.02	PL	Chelsea	A	D 2-2	1
27.08.02	EC	Zalaegerszeg	H	W 5-0	1
31.08.02	PL	Sunderland	A	D 1-1	=
03.09.02	PL	Middlesbrough	A	W 1-0	=
11.09.02	PL	Bolton Wanderers	H	L 0-1	-
14.09.02	PL	Leeds United	A	L 0-1	-
18.09.02	EC	Maccabi Haifa	H	W 5-2	-
21.09.02	PL	Tottenham H	H	W 1-0	-
24.09.02	EC	B Leverkusen	A	W 2-1	-
28.09.02	PL	Charlton Athletic	A	W 3-1	-
01.10.02	EC	Olympiakos	H	W 4-0	-
07.10.02	PL	Everton	H	W 3-0	-

For *ENGLAND*

12.10.02	ECQ	Slovakia	A	W 2-1	1
16.10.02	ECQ	Macedonia	H	D 2-2	1

For *MANCHESTER UNITED*

19.10.02	PL	Fulham	A	D 1-1	-
23.10.02	EC	Olympiakos	A	W 3-2	-
26.10.02	PL	Aston Villa	H	D 1-1	-
02.11.02	PL	Southampton	H	W 2-1	-
05.11.02	LC	Leicester City	H	W 2-0	1
13.11.02	EC	B Leverkusen	H	W 2-0	-
11.12.02	EC	La Coruna	H	W 2-0	=
14.12.02	PL	West Ham United	H	W 3-0	-
17.12.02	LC	Chelsea	H	W 1-0	-
22.12.02	PL	Blackburn Rovers	A	L 0-1	-
26.12.02	PL	Middlesbrough	A	L 1-3	-
28.12.02	PL	Birmingham City	H	W 2-0	1
01.01.03	PL	Sunderland	H	W 2-1	1
04.01.03	FA	Portsmouth	H	W 4-1	1
07.01.03	LC	Blackburn Rovers	H	D 1-1	-
11.01.03	PL	West Brom	A	W 3-1	-
18.01.03	PL	Chelsea	H	W 2-1	-
22.01.03	LC	Blackburn Rovers	A	W 3-1	-
26.01.03	FA	West Ham United	H	W 6-0	-
01.02.03	PL	Southampton	A	W 2-0	-
04.02.03	PL	Birmingham City	A	W 1-0	-
09.02.03	PL	Manchester City	H	D 1-1	-

For *ENGLAND*

12.02.03	FR	Australia	H	L 1-3	-

For *MANCHESTER UNITED*

15.02.03	FA	Arsenal	H	L 0-2	-
19.02.03	EC	Juventus	H	W 2-1	-
22.02.03	PL	Bolton Wanderers	A	D 1-1	-
25.02.03	EC	Juventus	A	W 3-0	-
02.03.03	LC	Liverpool	A	L 0-2	-
05.03.03	PL	Leeds United	H	W 2-1	-
12.03.03	EC	Basle	H	D 1-1	-
15.03.03	PL	Aston Villa	A	W 1-0	1
22.03.03	PL	Fulham	H	W 3-0	-

For *ENGLAND*

29.03.03	ECQ	Liechtenstein	A	W 2-0	1
02.04.03	ECQ	Turkey	H	W 2-0	1

For *MANCHESTER UNITED*

05.04.03	PL	Liverpool	H	W 4-0	-
08.04.03	EC	Real Madrid	A	L 1-3	-
19.04.03	PL	Blackburn Rovers	H	W 3-1	-
23.04.03	EC	Real Madrid	H	W 4-3	2
27.04.03	PL	Tottenham H	A	W 2-0	-
03.05.03	PL	Charlton Athletic	H	W 4-1	1
11.05.03	PL	Everton	A	W 2-1	1

For *ENGLAND*

22.05.03	FR	South Africa	A	W 2-1	-

Date	Comp	Opponents	Venue	Result	FW Goals
For ENGLAND					
20.08.03	FR	Croatia	H	W 3-1	1
For REAL MADRID					
24.08.03	SSC	Mallorca	A	L 1-2	-
27.08.03	SSC	Mallorca	H	W 3-0	1
30.08.03	LL	Real Betis	H	W 1-2	1
02.09.03	LL	Villareal	H	D 1-1	-
For ENGLAND					
06.09.03	ECQ	Macedonia	A	W 2-1	1
10.09.03	ECQ	Leichtenstein	H	W 2-0	-
For REAL MADRID					
13.09.03	LL	Valladolid	H	W 7-2	-
16.09.03	CL	Marseille	H	W 4-2	-
21.09.03	LL	Malaga	A	W 3-1	1
27.09.03	LL	Valencia	A	L 0-2	-
05.10.03	LL	Espanyol	H	W 2-1	-
For ENGLAND					
11.10.03	ECQ	Turkey	A	D 0-0	-
For REAL MADRID					
18.10.03	LL	Celta Vigo	A	W 2-0	-
22.10.03	ECL	P Belgrade	H	W 1-0	-
01.11.03	LL	At Bilbao	H	W 3-0	-
04.11.03	ECL	P Belgrade	A	D 0-0	-
09.11.03	LL	Sevilla	A	L 1-4	-
For ENGLAND					
16.11.03	FR	Denmark	H	L 2-3	-
For REAL MADRID					
23.11.03	LL	Albecete	H	W 2-1	1
26.11.03	ECL	Marseille	A	W 2-1	1
29.11.03	LL	Osasuna	A	D 1-1	-
03.12.03	LL	Atl Madrid	H	W 2-0	-
06.12.03	LL	Barcelona	A	W 2-1	-
14.12.03	LL	La Coruna	H	W 2-1	-
03.01.04	LL	Murcia	H	W 1-0	-
18.01.04	LL	Real Betis	A	D 1-1	-
24.01.04	LL	Villareal	H	W 2-1	-
01.02.04	LL	Valladolid	A	W 3-2	-
07.02.04	LL	Malaga	H	W 2-1	-
15.02.04	LL	Valencia	H	D 1-1	-
For ENGLAND					
18.02.04	Fr	Portugal	A	D 1-1	-
For REAL MADRID					
24.02.04	ECL	Bayern Munich	A	D 1-1	-
29.02.04	LL	Celta Vigo	H	W 4-2	-
06.03.04	LL	Santander	A	D 1-1	-
10.03.04	ECL	Bayern Munich	H	W 1-0	-
13.03.04	LL	Real Zaragoza	H	D 1-1	-
20.03.04	LL	Ath Bilbao	A	L 2-4	-
24.03.04	ECL	Monaco	H	W 4-2	-
28.03.04	LL	Seville	H	W 5-1	-
03.04.04	LL	Albacete	A	L 1-2	-
11.04.04	LL	Osasuna	H	L 0-3	-
17.04.04	LL	At Madrid	A	W 2-1	-
25.04.04	LL	Barcelona	H	L 1-2	-
01.05.04	LL	La Coruna	A	L 0-2	-
08.05.04	LL	Mallorca	H	L 2-3	-
16.05.04	LL	Murcia	H	L 0-1	-
For ENGLAND					
01.06.04	Fr	Japan	H	D 1-1	-
05.06.04	Fr	Iceland	H	W 6-1	-
13.06.04	ECF	France	N	L 1-2	-
17.06.04	ECF	Switzerland	N	W 3-0	-
21.06.04	ECF	Croatia	N	w 4-2	-
24.06.04	ECF	Portugal	A	d 2-2*	-
(*Portugal won on penalties)					

SEASON 2004-05

Date	Comp	Opponents	Venue	Result	
For *ENGLAND*					
18.08.04	FR	Ukraine	H	W 3-0	1
For *REAL MADRID*					
29.08.04	LL	Mallorca	A	W 1-0	-
For *ENGLAND*					
04.09.04	WCQ	Austria	A	D 2-2	-
08.09.04	WCQ	Poland	A	W 2-1	-
For *REAL MADRID*					
11.09.04	LL	Numancia	H	W 1-0	1
15.09.04	ECL	B Leverkusen	A	L 0-3	-
18.09.04	LL	Espanyol	A	L 0-1	-
21.09.05	LL	Osasuna	H	W 1-0	1
25.09.04	LL	At Bilbao	A	L 1-2	-
28.09.04	ECL	Roma	H	W 4-2	-
03.10.04	LL	La Coruna	H	L 0-1	-
For *ENGLAND*					
09.10.04	WCQ	Wales	H	W 2-0	1
For *REAL MADRID*					
14.11.04	LL	Albacete	H	W 6-1	-
For *ENGLAND*					
17.11.04	FR	Spain	A	L 0-1	-
For *REAL MADRID*					
20.11.04	LL	Barcelona	A	L 0-3	-
23.11.04	ECL	B Leverkusen	H	D 1-1	-
28.11.04	LL	Levante	H	W 5-0	1
05.12.04	LL	Villareal	A	D 0-0	-
08.12.04	ECL	Roma	A	W 3-0	-
22.12.04	LL	Seville	H	L 0-1	-
05.01.05	LL	Real Sociedad	H	W 2-1	-
09.01.05	LL	Atl Madrid	A	W 3-0	-
16.01.05	LL	Real Zaragoza	H	W 3-1	-
23.01.05	LL	Mallorca	H	W 3-1	-
30.01.05	LL	Numancia	A	W 2-1	1
05.02.05	LL	Espanyol	H	W 4-0	-
For *ENGLAND*					
09.02.05	FR	Holland	H	D 0-0	-
For *REAL MADRID*					
13.02.05	LL	Osasuna	A	W 2-1	-
19.02.05	LL	At Bilbao	H	L 0-2	-
22.02.05	ECL	Juventus	H	W 1-0	-
26.02.05	LL	La Coruna	A	L 0-2	-
02.03.05	LL	Real Betis	H	W 3-1	-
05.03.05	LL	Valencia	A	D 1-1	-
09.03.05	ECL	Juventus	A	L 0-2	-
20.03.05	LL	Malaga	H	W 1-0	-
For *ENGLAND*					
26.03.05	WCQ	N Ireland	H	W 4-0	-
30.03.05	WCQ	Azerbaijan	H	W 2-0	1
For *REAL MADRID*					
10.04.05	LL	Barcelona	H	W 4-2	-
17.04.05	LL	Levante	A	W 2-0	-
24.04.05	LL	Villareal	H	W 2-1	-
30.04.05	LL	Real Sociedad	A	W 2-0	-
07.05.05	LL	Santander	H	W 5-0	-
14.05.05	LL	Seville	A	D 2-2	-
21.05.05	LL	Atl Madrid	H	D 0-0	-
For *ENGLAND*					
31.05.05	FR	Colombia	N	W 3-2	-

Favourite Beckham Moments

What are your top memories of
David's career?

DATE: _AUGUST 4th1 3th 2008_

COMPETITION: _____

OPPONENTS: _____

VENUE: _____

RESULT: _____

WHY WAS THIS MATCH SO SPECIAL?

_____
_____
_____
_____
_____
_____

Puzzle Solutions

SPOT THE DIFFERENCES – Page 38

LA LIGA WORD SEARCH – Page 47

NAME THE PLAYERS – Page 39

A: Teddy Sheringham

B: Steven Gerrard

C: John Terry

D: Luis Figo

E: Rio Ferdinand

DB X-WORD – Page 49

DB QUIZ – Page 48

Answers...

1. Six

2. Los Galacticos

3. In Germany

4. 1992

5. Taurus

6. Leeds United

7. 1999

8. Ireland

9. Neil Sullivan, of Wimbledon

10. Portugal

11. Cheshunt, in Hertfordshire

12. Jonathan Woodgate

13. Joseph

14. His 30th

15. Michael Owen

16. Italy

17. Caroline

18. Preston (he was on loan)

19. Gary Peters

20. 'Beckingham Palace'